IN DEFENSE OF FREEDOM
and Related Essays

Frank S. Meyer
(1909–1972)

Frank S. Meyer

IN DEFENSE
OF FREEDOM
and Related
Essays

WITH A FOREWORD BY

WILLIAM C. DENNIS

Liberty Fund
Indianapolis

This book is published by Liberty Fund, Inc., a foundation established to encourage study of the ideal of a society of free and responsible individuals.

The cuneiform inscription that serves as our logo and as the design motif for our endpapers is the earliest-known written appearance of the word "freedom" (*amagi*), or "liberty." It is taken from a clay document written about 2300 B.C. in the Sumerian city-state of Lagash.

04 15 16 17 18 19 20 21 C 8   7   6   5   4   3   2
15 16 17 18 19 20 21 22 P 12   11   10   9   8   7   6

Library of Congress Cataloging-in-Publication Data

Meyer, Frank S.
    In defense of freedom and related essays / Frank S. Meyer ; with a foreword by William C. Dennis.
      p.   cm.
    Includes bibliographical references and index.
    ISBN 978-0-86597-139-4 (hardcover).--ISBN 978-0-86597-140-0 (pbk)
    1. Conservatism.   2. Conservatism—United States.   I. Title.
JC573.M49   1996
320.5'2'0973—dc20   95-39943
                                             CIP

Liberty Fund, Inc.
8335 Allison Pointe Trail, Suite 300
Indianapolis, IN 46250-1684

Our band is few, but true and tried,
our leader frank and bold . . .

> —William Cullen Bryant,
> "Song of Marion's Men"

Firm, united, let us be,
Rallying round our Liberty;
As a band of brothers joined,
Peace and safety we shall find.

> —Joseph Hopkinson,
> "Hail, Columbia"

These epigraphs are taken from *Breathes There the Man: Heroic Ballads and Poems of the English-Speaking Peoples*, edited by Frank S. Meyer.

Contents

PART THREE

RELATED ESSAYS

PART FOUR

CODA

Foreword

Frank Straus Meyer was a leader in the founding generation of post–World War II American conservatism. Like Whittaker Chambers, Max Eastman, and John Dos Passos, he embraced conservatism after having been a member of the Communist Party, and like them, too, Meyer became a fierce and unrelenting foe of communism and the Soviet Union that sponsored its spread worldwide. In addition, Meyer was the key figure of the 1950s and 1960s who argued that American conservatives should not let factional ideological quarrels distract them from their duty to further their common heritage of liberty and to reduce the power of the Leviathan state. Meyer's *In Defense of Freedom: A Conservative Credo*, the most philosophical and least polemical of his works, is the defining statement of this belief. The work is his enduring intellectual legacy.[1]

Meyer was born on May 9, 1909, in Newark, New Jersey, to Jack F. Meyer, a New York lawyer, and Helene Straus Meyer. He

---

1. Frank S. Meyer, *In Defense of Freedom: A Conservative Credo* (Chicago: Henry Regnery, 1962). The dedications in each of Meyer's books reflect his most important loyalties. *In Defense of Freedom* contains the dedication: "To L. Brent Bozell, William F. Buckley, Jr., Willmoore Kendall. Companions in battle. Whetstones of the mind. None of whom will by any means agree with much of this book; without whom, however, it could not have been written." All page references to *In Defense of Freedom* and the related essays are to the previously published versions; references to the same works in this Liberty Fund collection follow in parentheses.

attended Princeton and then Balliol College, Oxford, where he received his B.A. in 1932 and his M.A. in 1934. While at Oxford he was a well-known radical student leader and secret member of the Communist Party, taking instruction from his party handlers on his duties as a student activist. This radical phase continued through his studies at the London School of Economics (1932–34) and at the University of Chicago (1934–38).[2] In 1940 Meyer married Elsie Bown, who became his life-long intellectual and political companion. They made their home on Ohayo Mountain Road in Woodstock, New York.[3] Here, over the years, the Meyers welcomed countless visitors for memorable nights of conversation, food and drink, and song. Their two sons are John C. and Eugene B. Meyer.[4]

Always the intellectual, Meyer, who turned to communism through a study of Marxist texts, began an agonizing reappraisal of his beliefs after reading F. A. Hayek's *The Road to Serf-*

2. Many years later, at a meeting of the Philadelphia Society, Meyer recounted tales of some of his party associates who still held various positions of influence.

3. Meyer's *The Moulding of Communists: The Training of the Communist Cadre* (New York: Harcourt, Brace, 1961) contains this dedication: "E. B. M. uxori meae quae mihi et in tenebris erranti et e tenebris exeunti eximia pietate animam confirmavit" (To my wife, who was with me while wandering in the darkness and who strengthened my spirit with her exceptional piety when I left it). Murray Rothbard wrote of the Meyers, "Never have I known two people so close, so intimate on every level; in this age of instability, here was a truly rare marriage, a marriage to cherish even for those of us who experienced it as friends." See Rothbard, "Frank S. Meyer, RIP," *Libertarian Forum,* May 1972, 8. William F. Buckley, Jr., wrote an obituary on Elsie Meyer. See Buckley, "Elsie Meyer, RIP," *National Review,* May 23, 1975, 546–47.

4. For sketches of the Meyers' life in Woodstock, see "Frank S. Meyer, RIP," *National Review,* April 28, 1972, 466–75. Contributors to this reminiscence were William F. Buckley, Jr., Peter P. Witonski, C. H. Simonds, Guy Davenport, James Burnham, M. Stanton Evans, Garry Wills, L. Brent Bozell, Neil McCaffrey, J. Daniel Mahoney, Jared Lobdell, Eliseo Vivas, Priscilla L. Buckley, and Hugh Kenner. Another fine biographical appreciation is Edwin J. Feulner's foreword to the Heritage Foundation's reprint of Meyer's "Freedom, Tradition, Conservatism," published as the *President's Essay, 1991.*

dom while serving in the U.S. Army during World War II.[5] In 1945, after fourteen years of active service at its direction, Meyer made a complete break with the party. In *The Moulding of Communists: The Training of the Communist Cadre,* a volume in the series Communism in American Life, edited by Clinton Rossiter, Meyer drew on his experiences as a party disciple to produce an important and chilling account of the role of the party, the cadre, and the ideology in creating and deploying the Communist revolutionary. This book is not an autobiographical recounting of Meyer's days as a Communist; nor is it a history of the American Communist movement. Instead, the book is a study of how the party in theory and practice went about creating the Communist man. Here Meyer showed how the Communists systematically attempted to transform the whole man—personality, intellect, and will—into a faithful servant of the party. For the fully developed Communist, there was to be no conceivable area of life in which Marxist-Leninist theory could not quickly provide certain and clarifying answers. Meyer's devotion to this systematic way of thought made it difficult for him to break with the party, even after he became convinced that Marxism was an intellectually puerile and hideous dogma.[6]

Meyer's intellectual pilgrimage from Marxism led eventually in 1955 to a position at the newly founded conservative magazine *National Review,* edited by William F. Buckley, Jr. Meyer became a senior editor of the magazine in 1957. "Principles and Heresies," a column Meyer wrote until his death, was one of the magazine's leading features. Meyer collected many of these columns, together with other of his writings, in *The Conservative Mainstream* (1969). In these columns, Meyer's writings ranged

5. "Champion of Freedom," *National Review,* May 7, 1960. This article is a review of F. A. Hayek's *The Constitution of Liberty* (Chicago: University of Chicago Press, 1960).

6. Meyer, *The Moulding of Communists,* 47–57, 156–58.

widely, covering contemporary domestic concerns, dangers abroad, moral decline, history, political philosophy, and the American political tradition. Among the topics he covered that remain of perennial interest are Abraham Lincoln; the future of the Republican Party; the sins of contemporary liberalism; foreign affairs and communism; and the nature of true education. This collection remains a revealing compendium of Meyer's views and concerns.[7]

During the last decade of his life, supported by small grants from various foundations, Meyer edited a newsletter entitled the *Exchange*. This periodical was a forum for discussion of academic and teaching issues and was a job-opening bulletin board for scholars on the Right. Circulation eventually grew to nearly one thousand. For several years after Meyer's death the *Exchange* continued under the editorship of Elsie Meyer, and after her death, under the auspices of the Intercollegiate Studies Institute.

Meyer's description of the Communist cadre was in some respects a self-portrait. He was a man of principle, devoted to sniffing out heresies wherever they might abide.[8] This ideological and partisan aspect of Meyer's life and work was manifested in his efforts on behalf of such conservative organizations as Young Americans for Freedom, the American Conservative Union, the Conservative Party of New York, and the Philadelphia Society. Meyer's character and convictions were further manifested in his support of the 1964 presidential campaign of Senator Barry Goldwater; in his support of Moise Tshombe's Katanga; in his hostility to Castro's Cuba, Khrushchev, nuclear disarmament, and liberal Republicans; and in his opposition to compulsory national service and the growing welfare state. Meyer pursued these principles and objectives with an energy

7. *The Conservative Mainstream* (New Rochelle, N.Y.: Arlington House, 1969). This book contains the dedication "To John and Eugene. In Hope."
8. "A Man of Principle" was Meyer's title for an early column on Barry Goldwater, *National Review*, April 23, 1960, 269–70.

and enthusiasm (laden with more than a touch of stridency) that endeared him to his followers but must have angered and outraged his adversaries. Only those who heard him speak publicly can have had a full appreciation of Meyer's singular embodiment of these principles. Fortunately, he spoke often, on college campuses, at meetings of the Philadelphia Society—where his spontaneous outbursts became legendary—or, for example, at the banquet commemorating the tenth anniversary of *National Review:*

> Conservatism is no more, nor less, than devotion to the restoration and renewal of the spirit of Western civilization. . . . The nature of men, firmly rooted in their creation, belies the constructions of the utopians. And when men set foot on the planets of Sirius or Vega they will still be men, not constructs. The natural habitat of man is freedom and piety towards the constitution of being, not subservience to a man-made utopian plan. By that token, however many battles we may lose, in the end the view of man and his relations to the universe for which we stand will triumph. But when, no man can say. We will have reverses and we will have successes. The road is a rough one. Still, I venture to predict, we will be back here ten years from now, ten years stronger, to signalize, fittingly, together the twentieth anniversary of *National Review* and the 200th anniversary of the War of Independence that launched our republic.[9]

Meyer's intellectual road from Marxist collectivism to the defense of individual liberty was paralleled by another, more drawn out, and evidently more wrenching spiritual journey that probably began during his days at Oxford. On the day of his death this proud Jew was baptized into the Catholic Church. As William F. Buckley, Jr., recounted after visiting Meyer on Good Friday, 1972: "The next day he was worse, much worse. That afternoon he saw Father [Eugene V.] Clark,

9. Transcribed by the editor from a recording of portions of the speeches presented at the dinner commemorating the tenth anniversary of *National Review* at the Imperial Ballroom of the Americana Hotel in New York City, November 11, 1965, National Review Recording NR-3, 1966.

and made the great submission, and a few hours later I was
called to the telephone. It was his son, Gene. I told him the
truth that his father was a great man, and hung up."[10]

The profound nature of this deathbed conversion renders
difficult an assessment of the importance of religion in Meyer's
earlier political thinking and writing. In the best published
study of Meyer's thought, Senator John P. East argued that the
key to understanding Frank Meyer "is to appreciate fully that
the Christian faith is the *summum bonum* of his thinking, and
that all other ideas flow from that fact and are corollaries to
it."[11] However, Meyer's own testimony suggests that the relationship of his political thought and Christianity was more
complicated and indirect than Senator East later suggested. In
his *In Defense of Freedom,* published a decade before his death,
Meyer wrote about "the constitution of being," "the eternal
order of truth," and "objective moral order" but not about
Christian virtue or God's grace, as East would have it. In a long
footnote, Meyer wrote that "Christianity, which informs Western civilization, is the highest and deepest relationship to the
Divine that men can attain, I am also certain; but I am not able
to say that any single institutional church is the bearer of God's
spirit. And this makes it impossible for me to discuss the
church in the terms of this book."[12] In answer to a question in
a November 1970 interview with John Boland, eventually published in the *New Guard,* the magazine of the Young Americans
for Freedom, Meyer described himself as having a "pretty complex theology" and as being a theist; essentially, though formally unattached, he accepted the Christian situation.[13]

10. *National Review,* April 28, 1972, 467.
11. John P. East, *The American Conservative Movement: The Philosophical Founders* (Chicago: Regnery Books, 1986), 71.
12. Meyer, *In Defense of Freedom,* 165 n (147 n).
13. Meyer said even more here: "I do believe in revelation, but I do not
believe in it being limited to a single document or a single church or anything
of the sort. What I really think, I guess—I'll try to work this out—is that

Meyer's *In Defense of Freedom: A Conservative Credo* was also
long in its development. He had published on the themes that
would inform this book at least as early as his short 1955 essay
"Collectivism Rebaptized."[14] Though *In Defense of Freedom* is not
a comprehensive philosophical treatise, it is a good primer for
each new generation's rediscovery of the tradition of liberty.[15]
In this book Meyer argued that American conservatism is a
blend of two strands of thought that for the most part remained in opposition to each other in Europe but in America
were historical and natural allies. On the one hand, there were
the "traditionalists," with their emphasis on value, virtue, and
order; on the other hand, there were the "libertarians," with
their stress upon freedom and the innate importance of the
individual. While British and Continental conservatism, concerned with religion, tradition, authority, ar d status, emerged
in reaction to the French Revolution, American conservatism
was a homegrown development; it combined a devotion to individual freedom with an appreciation for the institutional arrangements of ordered liberty that made the practice of
freedom possible. For Meyer the individualism of the libertarians made no philosophical sense without an implicit acceptance of some "absolute ground of value . . . [while] the belief

---

through a steady growth of civilization—ups and downs, obviously not steady;
I'm a bit Spenglerian and think of civilizations rising and falling—but through
civilization and especially through Western civilization in its total works, as it
were, a revelation exists." See John Boland, "An Interview with Frank S. Meyer,"
New Guard (July/August 1975): 6–8. See also Meyer's "Western Civilization: The
Problem of Political Freedom," *Modern Age* (Spring 1968): 120–28, reprinted
herein (209–24).

14. *Freeman* (July 1955): 559–62. Reprinted in this collection (3–13).

15. John P. East's excellent summary may be found in *The American Conservative Movement*, 75–88. Meyer's own best short statement is "Freedom, Tradition, Conservatism," *Modern Age* (Fall 1960): 355–63. A slightly longer version
of this essay may be found in *What Is Conservatism?* (New York: Holt, Rinehart
and Winston, 1964), 7–20, reprinted herein (14–29). This book contains the
dedication: "*In memoriam:* Richard M. Weaver, pioneer and protagonist of the
American conservative consensus."

in virtue as the end of men's being implicitly recognizes the necessity of freedom to choose that end. . . ."[16]

But why freedom? Because, Meyer argued, freedom is the quality that separates men from other orders of the universe. Freedom to make choices is at the center of "the drama of human existence."[17] Society and the state, then, are instrumental; they are not purposeful or moral orders. The value of these institutions depends on the degree to which they facilitate individuals in the pursuit of their own purposes. According to Meyer, the locus of virtue is in the individual, and the individual to be truly human must be free to choose, even if he chooses in error. "Only if there exists a real choice between right and wrong, truth and error, a choice which can be made irrespective of the direction in which history and impersonal Fate move, do men possess true freedom."[18]

From this line of argument, Meyer concluded that the advancement of individual liberty should be the highest duty of the politician. Though the political realm cannot compel virtuous action, it can provide the conditions in which the free man can best pursue virtue on his own. Yet political theorists of collectivist liberalism, the liberalism of the New Deal, and the emerging New Conservatism of the 1950s had abandoned the American political ideal of liberty. Collectivists did so in the name of social science. The New Conservatives—identified by Meyer as those of the 1950s who deemed themselves to be the intellectual heirs of Edmund Burke and several nineteenth-century conservatives[19]—did so in the name of tradition. In Meyer's judgment, each group had subordinated the individual to the collective and had, therefore, reduced men to something less than human. "Neither the welfare statist with his

---

16. Meyer, "Freedom, Tradition, Conservatism," 9 (16).
17. Meyer, *In Defense of Freedom*, 22 (47).
18. Ibid., 49 (67).
19. See Meyer, *In Defense of Freedom*, 2–4 (34–35), for a description of his limited meaning for this term.

materialist ends nor the New Conservative with his spiritual ends is willing to accept freedom," said Meyer.[20]

This strong, explicit attack on the New Conservatism of the 1950s made *In Defense of Freedom* a controversial book. The thrust of the controversy was Meyer's insistence that the New Conservatives had forgotten the essential nature of the tradition they claimed to be defending. Prudential choice among "immediate practical alternatives" was a proper stance for the enlightened statesman, but, Meyer argued, conservative intellectuals could not depend on "prescription" and "Providential dispensation" to defend the liberties of the West against collectivist doctrines. Reason and judgment needed to be used to preserve and develop the institutions and ideals of freedom once they had emerged in the course of history and had proved themselves to be good for mankind.[21]

In contrast to the New Conservatives, therefore, Meyer called for a "conservatism of principle," or "a conscious conservatism," and argued that men needed to face up to the shock of freedom. "Freedom brings men rudely and directly face to face with their own personal responsibility for their own free actions."[22] This confrontation may present a serious challenge to modern men. Collectivism of one sort or another has dominated our political culture for so long that the constituency for liberty appears to be diminished. Even so, Meyer entertained no doubts about his objective or of the possibility of renewed devotion to freedom in America. Sounding a populist note, he maintained until the last that, though the political order had become corrupted, "the old truths, the old understanding still live in the hearts, the basic moral instincts, the fundamental beliefs of ordinary Americans."[23] He devoted *In Defense of Freedom* to showing how his understanding of rights,

20. Ibid., 60 (74).
21. Ibid., 40–48 (60–66).
22. Ibid., 169 (150).
23. Ibid., 170 (150).

virtue, order, the good society, and the dangers of the modern
Leviathan state is connected to his thesis that personal and political freedom stand at the center of the American political
tradition.

Meyer's argument that freedom is the basis of virtue, and
not the other way around, and his belief that there is an essential harmony between American conservatism and libertarianism, were immediately controversial—and they still are
controversial. Other thinkers were immediate and pointed in
response, and Meyer was equally pointed in engaging his chal-
lengers and critics. Eventually these exchanges would encom-
pass an extensive polemical literature, constituting an ongoing
conversation among many of the leading lights of post–World
War II conservative or libertarian thought, including Russell
Kirk, Father Stanley Parry, John Hallowell, L. Brent Bozell,
Willmoore Kendall, Ronald Hamowy, Murray Rothbard, Felix
Morley, Richard Weaver, M. Stanton Evans, Donald J. Devine,
Stephen Tonsor, and Peter Stanlis.[24] Several of the essays im-
portant to this debate were reprinted in *What Is Conservatism?*
The effects of this controversy linger today in a cacophony of
conservative voices that have succeeded the libertarians and
New Conservatives of Meyer's generation.

Today, as before, the issue is, as George H. Nash has written,
"nothing less than the intellectual legitimacy of the coalition
that had developed in the mid-1950s. . . . Did libertarians and
traditionalists really have any business associating with one another?"[25] Meyer convinced few of his adversaries in his own day
that they did—that his reconciliation of the best parts of con-

24. For a full description of the controversy engendered by *In Defense of
Freedom*, see George H. Nash, *The Conservative Intellectual Movement in America
Since 1945* (New York: Basic Books, 1976), especially chapters 5 and 6, and
East, *The American Conservative Movement*, 75–81, 96–101. Nash is especially
good in describing the many intellectual streams in the controversy between
Meyer and his conservative and libertarian contemporaries and he also pro-
vides a fine personal portrait of Meyer.

25. Nash, *The Conservative Intellectual Movement*, 172.

servative traditionalism with a libertarianism based in American history could be sustained. He was, however, the first to insist that such a unity was not only possible but also necessary considering the political crisis at home and the dangers of communism abroad. Yet for many readers Meyer's fusionism (as it was called by his friendly adversary L. Brent Bozell) will remain convincing simply because it makes such good sense and because the readers believe Meyer described the true nature of American conservatism as they have come to know it through their own experience and study.[26] For these readers it will not be Meyer's text that seems narrow and doctrinaire, but rather those of his uncompromising libertarian and traditionalist critics—the first group irrational in their arid rationalism, the second unaware of the realities of their own tradition.

What would Meyer make of the world that came into being after the collapse of the Soviet empire? Edwin J. Feulner, president of the Heritage Foundation, speculated that "Frank would have rejoiced not only in the triumph of freedom, but also in the way it has happened—with whole societies—one man, one heart, one spirit at a time refusing to acquiesce in iniquity, refusing to be the commissar's creature. . . ."[27] This much is surely true. In a moving essay, typically full of passion and exuberance, published in *National Review,* January 1961, Meyer wrote of his hope that the world would soon witness a new birth of liberty. He argued that for the first time in modern America an intellectual conservatism was arising and that it was beginning to put collectivist liberalism on the defensive throughout the humane disciplines of American university faculties:

> I do not want to exaggerate. I am not maintaining that the stranglehold of the arid and nihilistic doctrines which for three genera-

---

26. Meyer discusses the use of the term "fusionism" in "Why Freedom," *National Review,* September 25, 1962, 223–25, and reprinted herein (155–63).

27. Edwin J. Feulner, Jr., *President's Essay* (Washington, D.C.: Heritage Foundation, 1991).

tions have increasingly permeated American thought is broken—
or even that it is on the verge of being broken. . . . What I do
maintain is that the tide has turned and turned unmistakably. . . . I
do not underestimate the hard, steel strength of power. Whether
for good or evil, it is power which has the next to the last word in
the affairs of men—but not the last word. . . . It is ideas and beliefs
that truly reflect the nature of man and his destiny that will in the
end decide our future.[28]

Meyer returned to this theme in the closing chapter of *In Defense of Freedom*: "Here lies the challenge to resurgent conservatism in America: simultaneously to create a new intellectual
and spiritual leadership, and on the basis of that leadership to
move forward to the defeat of collectivist liberalism in the political sphere."[29]

Despite its partisan conclusion, Meyer did not intend for *In
Defense of Freedom* to be read in some narrow, particularistic fashion. He believed his message would appeal to all who gave him a
thoughtful ear, because he thought there was a common interest in the maintenance of a free society. For Meyer, a social order was a good order to the degree that it permitted men to live
in freedom under conditions in which virtue could be advanced
and perpetuated. And he believed that America had been, and
should continue to be, such a society. Of course, freedom has its
risks because vice, not virtue, might characterize man's advance.
But, then, all existence has its risks. Unless men can choose to
be vicious, they cannot act to be virtuous. And, while a community may be able to compel good behavior, compulsion does not
produce virtuous men.[30] Armed with this understanding, both
the serious student of liberty and the activist in the cause of freedom would be well prepared for further work.

A fair-minded look at the history of the past twenty years
would lead to the conclusion that only a part of Meyer's vision

28. *The Conservative Mainstream,* "Hope for the '60s," 87–88.
29. Meyer, *In Defense of Freedom,* 170–71 (150–51).
30. Ibid., 166 (147–48).

has been realized. Indeed, defeats in some areas may have balanced gains in others. But one can be sure that Meyer would continue to glory in the intellectual and polemical struggle on behalf of freedom. In an oft-quoted observation on Meyer, Whittaker Chambers wrote to William F. Buckley, Jr.:

> If the Rep. Party [and evidently conservatives in general] cannot get some grip of the actual world we live in and from it generalize and actively promote a program that means something to the masses of people—why, somebody else will. There will be nothing to argue. The voters will simply vote Republicans into singularity. The Rep. Party will become like one of those dark shops which apparently never sell anything. If, for any reason, you go in, you find, at the back, an old man, fingering for his own pleasure, some oddments of cloth (weave and design of 1850). Nobody wants to buy them, which is fine because the old man is not really interested in selling. He just likes to hold and to feel. As your eyes become accustomed to the dim kerosene light, you are only slightly surprised to see that the old man is Frank Meyer.[31]

In one sense these lines do describe the Meyer of Woodstock. Yet, as the passage of time has shown, Chambers's characterization of Meyer assuredly is flawed. True, Meyer would not yield to the *Zeitgeist*, but he did not despair that the reforms he advocated were possible politically. He devoted his life to the unending task of changing the nature of the political order so that it would correspond more to the truth of "the great tradition of the West"[32]—or as he liked to put it, to the "constitution of being." In contrast to Chambers's description, then, such a man had a great deal that he was eager to sell. Still today we may find his old cloth to be woven from threads of gold.

William C. Dennis

---

31. *Odyssey of a Friend: Whittaker Chambers's Letters to William F. Buckley, Jr., 1954–1961,* edited by William F. Buckley, Jr. (New York: G. P. Putnam's Sons, 1970), 216.

32. Meyer, "Freedom, Tradition, Conservatism," 9 (16).

PART ONE

PRELUDE

Collectivism Rebaptized

When two or three years ago Russell Kirk, then a member of the faculty of Michigan State College, published a volume called *The Conservative Mind*, he hardly expected, it is to be presumed, that within a short time it would make him the major prophet of a flourishing new movement. But the emergence of the New Conservatism, which has for some time filled the columns of the quarterlies and magazines of opinion and is now spilling out into the larger world, can indeed be accurately correlated with the appearance of that book.

There were, it is true, earlier premonitions—the shrill cries of Peter Viereck, scattered articles here and there on a more urbane pitch, and other books of the serious caliber of Dr. Kirk's own writing, such as Robert A. Nisbet's *The Quest for Community.* But it was *The Conservative Mind* which precipitated the New Conservatism.

The speed of its development has been enormous, even for a time like ours, when ideas are packaged into trends and movements long before they have had a chance to cure properly. Within the past year or so a multitude of books has appeared, carrying the general theme. To mention only a few, Dr. Kirk himself has produced two more volumes (in descending order

Reprinted from *Freeman* (July 1955): 559–62, by permission.

of quality, as he grapples with more concrete problems), *A Program for Conservatives* and *Academic Freedom*. Walter Lippmann in *The Public Philosophy* has jumped on the bandwagon, although without explicit acknowledgment, giving a more journalistic twist and more practical momentum to the movement. And the real proof that Dr. Kirk's donnish speculations have brought forth a gusher is the recent appearance, under the aegis of a publisher whose scent for current intellectual fashion is second to none and with the seal of approval of the Charles Austin Beard Prize, of *Conservatism in America* by Clinton Rossiter. This book, hailed as "an eloquent appeal for a new conservatism to sustain the Republic in the troubled years ahead," presents nothing in its essential principles and program with which Arthur Schlesinger, Jr., or Adlai Stevenson would seriously disagree.

This fundamental compatibility with the collectivist trend of the time which comes out so blatantly in Mr. Rossiter has been implicit in the New Conservatism from the beginning, despite much just and tonic criticism of positivist ethics and the blatant centralizing *tone* of the "liberal" atmosphere by Russell Kirk and his more serious colleagues. Why, then, the tendency, in circles usually strongly critical of collectivism, to receive the New Conservatism as a valid theoretical foundation for a movement of opposition to it?

This is perhaps partly a matter of words, of labels. The term "liberal" has for some time now been captured by the proponents of a powerful state and a controlled economy and has been corrupted into the opposite of its true meaning. To be conservative has, therefore, by usage and consent come to mean to be an opponent of that false "liberalism." From a certain point of view there has been logic to this custom, when by conservative was understood loyalty to the established traditions of the Constitution and to a free American social structure, as over against the Roosevelt revolution.

A Difference of Principle

In fact, conservatism is not a body of principles, but a tone, an attitude. That attitude does indeed tend to conduce towards a respect for the wisdom acquired by human beings through long ages and towards skepticism of social blueprints, of utopias, of the approach of the Socialist and the social worker. It carries with it, however, no built-in defense against the acceptance, grudging though it may be, of institutions which reason and prudence would otherwise reject, if only those institutions are sufficiently firmly established.

The fundamental political issue today is that between, on the one hand, collectivism and statism which merge gradually into totalitarianism and, on the other, what used to be called liberalism, what we may perhaps call individualism: the principles of the primacy of the individual, the division of power, the limitation of government, the freedom of the economy. This is not a problem of tone or attitude, not a difference between the conservative and the radical temperament; *it is a difference of principle.* What is at stake are fundamental concepts of the relationship of individual men to a society and the institutions of a society.

On this issue, Dr. Kirk, and others who are seriously interested in the fundamental questions which concern him, are at the best equivocal, while the more journalistic New Conservatives, Viereck, Lippmann, Rossiter, seize upon the attitude of conservatism to justify conservation of—the New Deal and its works. This kind of conservative must, in Clinton Rossiter's words, reject the "indecent anti-statism of laissez-faire individualism." For the New Conservative must not forget man's "need for both voluntary and submissive association with other men. The individualism of the Right has not been an inspiration for all Americans, but a clever weapon with which the rich could defend their riches and the powerful their power."

"Liberalism" is wearing a bit thin, fraying at the edges. Provided the fundamental realities of power—group and state over the individual, "sober community responsibility" over "laissez-faire anarchy"—are retained (and consolidated), the mantle of the conservative tone can well befit the established order of the welfare society. After all, that order is in its twenty-third year since the fateful election of 1932. The New Conservatism is, on an intellectual level, a natural complement to the Eisenhower version of Rooseveltism. Conservatism, after all, is a relative term. The question is: what do you want to conserve?

What, then, do the New Conservatives want to conserve? What is the content of their position and the principles for which they stand? To answer that question in a brief article requires at the best some simplification. There are different men and different emphases among the New Conservatives. It would hardly be fair to take as representative Clinton Rossiter's vulgarizations of the New Conservatism, or the tired platitudes of Walter Lippmann, or the strident diatribes of Peter Viereck as his New Conservatism leads him to the glorification of Adlai Stevenson. However a doctrine may be perverted or misused, its essential value stands or falls on its own merit. That it can be misused is of course a primary reason for examining very carefully its pretensions; but in the end, whatever is made of them, it is the ideas themselves with which we have to come to grips.

The Thinking of Russell Kirk

Therefore, it is to the effective thinkers of the movement that analysis and criticism should be directed. Of these Russell Kirk is undoubtedly the most significant. But it is not an easy matter to pin down Dr. Kirk's thinking. There is no doubt as to his general tone and attitude nor as to the source and content of his ultimate values; but in the field of human action—the area of ethics, politics, and economics—it is almost impossible to find clear and distinct principle.

To suggest the quality of his tone, one can perhaps do no better than to quote Dr. Kirk himself: "Now, in sober reality, conservatives are . . . a number of persons, of all classes and occupations, whose view of life is reverential, and who tend to be guided by the wisdom of their ancestors, instead of abstract speculation."

The source of his ultimate values is the accumulated wisdom of Western civilization, impinging upon his imagination most strongly, it would seem, in the forms achieved by the English eighteenth and nineteenth centuries and with the spiritual content of High Anglican Christianity. Those ultimate values can be and have been the starting point for many modes of action in the world, but integrally they lead to a belief in the unique value of every individual person, a belief which is the first principle of any philosophy of freedom (and which can, of course, also be arrived at in other ways).

But it is only the first principle. However deeply it is held, it is not by itself sufficient to guarantee the freedom of men in society. Too many interpretations are possible as to what the "integrity of the individual person" consists of. And, given the persuasiveness of one of these interpretations, men will always be found who, if they possess the power, will attempt to enforce their interpretation on other men. The only way the freedom of individuals can be protected against this ever-present danger is through a second set of principles. While these principles have for their aim the actualization of the philosophical and spiritual end, the freedom and integrity of the individual, they are themselves derived not only from this end but also from the realities of human life. They are framed with full awareness of the propensity of human beings to translate the freedom of other human beings into their freedom to do what those with power think is right and just.

In the ethical, the political, the economic spheres, these

practical principles are as vital as the general philosophical principle, if freedom is to be transformed from a dream into the actual situation in which men live. They can be rather simply stated, and they are the criteria by which the pretensions of a political philosophy, by whatever name it calls itself, must be judged.

The first of these principles is no more than the restatement of the innate value of the individual person in political and social terms: *all* value resides in the individual; *all* social institutions derive their value and, in fact, their very being from individuals and are justified only to the extent that they serve the needs of individuals.

From this fundamental axiom of the good society are developed two others which arise from experience and from understanding of the dangers to freedom which lie in the very nature of human beings. Since power is the instrumentality of control by men and groups of men over other men and since in this imperfect world, in the end, the only check upon power is power, the division of power (both within the political sphere and between the political sphere and other spheres) and unceasing vigilance to keep it divided are the essential safeguards of freedom.

With this goes the other and corollary principle, a special case of the principle of division of power, but of the greatest importance: the entire sphere of economic activity must remain free of political control. For only the strict separation of the sources of a man's material existence—property, employment, provision for illness and old age—from political institutions can enable him to maintain his independence of them. And further, if the state, which is the legal repository of force for the preservation of the conditions of peaceful civil life and for defense against external enemies, gains control over any other sphere of human activity, the very possibility of effective division of power is gone.

Rejects the Tradition of Individualism

If Dr. Kirk's thinking is judged by these principles, it becomes apparent that he lacks the standards to effectuate politically and socially his undoubtedly genuine concern for the integrity of the individual person as a philosophical and spiritual truth. He can criticize with great cogency the dehumanizing aspects of the federal social security program. He can stigmatize the totalitarian implications of the federal school lunch program. But on these, as on a dozen other practical issues of growing collectivism and the state's encroachment, he shows no sign of understanding the problems of principle reflected. He can write feelingly of the dangers of concentration of power without ever indicating by what standards overconcentration is to be judged and to what limits it is to be restrained. His books are full of just and shrewd critiques of aspect after aspect of the contemporary world, but for every such critique there is, implied or explicit, a condemnation of the ideas and the institutional frameworks which are essential to the reversal of the trend.

Nor is he merely neutral or undecided in his attitude towards these principles. Once they are stated clearly and unequivocally, he castigates them as the abstractions of "defecated intellectuals." He detests them and the men who formulated them and the whole tradition of individualism as heartily as he does Marxism and contemporary materialist collectivism.

If Dr. Kirk is so concerned about the evils he sees around us, the fruits of developing collectivism, and nevertheless rejects the principles of a free society, what does he propose, what does he stand for positively? Since he presents himself and his beliefs always rhetorically, never on a reasoned basis, he can succeed in establishing the impression that he has a strong and coherent outlook without ever taking a systematic and consistent position. In justice to him, it must be said that he would

make a virtue of this. He pours scorn on all the systematic positions he discusses as being "abstract," "radical," "Jacobin,"
"liberal"; and he exalts, as the model of conservative states-
manship, disdain for systematic thought and respect for "prejudice and prescription," that is, for the traditionally accepted.

Dr. Kirk takes as his guide the English statesman, Edmund
Burke, and puts him forward as the paragon of conservatism.
But what he forgets is that Burke was fighting against the radical principles of centralization of the French Revolution in defense of a society whose traditions themselves incorporated a
systematic, if incomplete, theory of freedom—the modes of
the common law, a considerable degree of division of power,
long-established rights of the individual and of property, the
principles of 1688. His reliance upon tradition, upon prescription, upon prejudice in the circumstances of 1790 would, in
the crisis of 1688, have made him the supporter of a very different policy and of very different principles. However much
one may respect Burke's stand as a practical statesman, it is
impossible to derive a firm political position from him. As
Richard Weaver has said: "Of clear rational principle he had a
mortal distrust . . . it would be blindness to take him as a
mentor."

It can be admitted that the long experience crystallized in
traditional human wisdom is a necessary make-weight to the
conclusions which reason would seem to dictate to a single
group or even to the conscience of a whole generation. But to
make tradition, "prejudice and prescription," not along with
reason but *against* reason, the sole foundation of one's position
is to enshrine the maxim, "Whatever is, is right," as the first
principle of thought about politics and society. Such a position
is immoral from any point of view; and actually Dr. Kirk could
not accept it, for it is particularly inconsonant with that Christian vision of the freedom of the soul and the will which he
holds. But we can only find what he does believe by strenuously
digging it out of the rhetorical flow. What he believes seems to

be that the particular strand of tradition which appeals to him, and which he presumptuously considers the only one compatible with Christianity, is right and is the only guide to a good society.

It will not imitate Dr. Kirk's own arrogance when he pontificates that "individualism is anti-Christian. It is possible logically to be a Christian, and possible logically to be an individualist; it is not possible to be the two simultaneously." No doubt his political position is compatible with Christianity, but so are many other positions. For Christianity, or any other religious vision, is concerned with the relations between the individual man and God. And while it certainly can, by affecting the inner being of individuals, affect the way in which they go about solving the problem of creating tolerable social conditions, it does not pretend to dictate a single form of these conditions valid for all ages and all times.

Dr. Kirk, however, seems to insist that a certain kind of society is the only tolerable one, and this not because *he* believes in it and puts forward arguments to support his concept. This certainly would be his privilege, however wrong he might be. But he pretends instead to have no principles personally arrived at. He merely recognizes what is ordained by Providential prescription.

The social pattern which emerges from the hints and suggestions in his writings (for he never tells us exactly what he wants and certainly never gives any idea of what it would mean in modern circumstances) is shaped by such words as "Authority," "order," "community," "duty," "obedience." "Freedom" is a rare word; "the individual" is anathema. The qualities of this suggested society are a mixture of those of eighteenth-century England and medieval Europe—or perhaps, more aptly, they are those of Plato's Republic with the philosopher-king replaced by the squire and the vicar.

No wonder that Dr. Kirk never describes concretely what such a society would be like under modern conditions, with the enormous strength of modern industry and modern arms, the decrease in distance and the ease of communication—in a word, with the technological facilities for power and centralization which exist today. Such societies of "authority and order," societies of status, have in the past, under the scattered and decentralized nature of power then, sometimes involved a considerable measure of freedom. But, quite apart from the essential and principled superiority of a society of contract to a society of status in terms of freedom, any society of status today, with the increased potentialities of power of our times, could only move inevitably to totalitarianism.

As all around us we see signs of regression from contract to status and the growing predominance of society and state over the individual, when this is indeed the characteristic form that the attack upon freedom takes today, Dr. Kirk in the peroration of *The Conservative Mind* can complacently write: "Our world may be passing from contract back to status. Whether that process is good or evil, conservatives must prepare society for Providential change. . . ."

If indeed our society ever completes the fearful voyage on which it has embarked "from contract back to status"—from freedom to slavery, not to put too fine a point upon it—it will not be the doing of Providence but of men. And alongside those men who have consciously substituted for the principles of freedom those of socialism and collectivism, the responsibility will be shared by those who, while they long for the conditions of our free ancestors, reject as abstract and doctrinaire the very principles which made them free. Dr. Kirk might well reread the passage from a speech of Randolph of Roanoke which begins the fourth chapter of his own book on that great statesman: "There are certain great principles, which if they be not held inviolate, at all seasons, our liberty is gone. If we give them up, it is perfectly immaterial what is the character of our Sovereign; whether he be King or President, elective or hereditary—it is perfectly immaterial what is his character—we shall be slaves. . . ."

Liberals Welcome New Conservatives

The "liberals" are well aware of all this. They realize that the New Conservatives, with their emphasis on tone and mood, with their lack of clear principle and their virulent rejection of individualism and a free economy, threaten no danger to the pillars of the temple. The conservative tone is indeed welcome now that power is to so large an extent achieved and the time come to consolidate and "conserve" it. Even better, by the magnanimity with which they receive the New Conservatives into polite society, they justify expelling into outer darkness the principled champions of limited government and a free economy as "crackpots" and "fringe elements."

They know their enemies. Their judgment is good. Only the principles of individual freedom—to Dr. Kirk the "conservatism of desolation"—can call a halt to the march of collectivism. The New Conservatism, stripped of its pretensions, is, sad to say, but another guise for the collectivist spirit of the age.

Freedom, Tradition,
Conservatism

The intellectual bankruptcy of the collectivist Liberalism which has dominated American thought for the past half century becomes every day more obvious. The imagination, the verve, the spiritual passion that once characterized it in its days of movement towards power have long since been replaced by a tired repetition of slogans empty of content and sustained only by the weight and inertia of bureaucratic power.

Power Liberalism still has beyond doubt, but power has only the next to the last word in the affairs of men—not the last word. Power is wielded by men, controlled by men, divided by men, limited by men, as they are guided and inspired by their intellectual and spiritual understanding. There may be a gap of years, of decades, between the onset of the impotence of a false world-view and the decay and defeat of the power structure which has arisen upon the foundations of that world-view. But its defeat is, given time, the necessary result of the reemergence of truth in the consciousness of those who are concerned with matters of the intellect, with matters of the spirit, of those who—though they may have little control over mate-

Reprinted from *What Is Conservatism?* (New York: Holt, Rinehart and Winston, for the Intercollegiate Studies Institute, 1964), by permission.

rial power at the moment—determine the foundations of the future.

The last half-dozen years have seen an intellectual revolt, unparalleled in a century, against the concepts upon which Liberal collectivism is based. It is ironic, although not historically unprecedented, that such a burst of creative energy on the intellectual level should occur simultaneously with a continuing spread of the influence of Liberalism in the practical political sphere, to the point where it has now captured the decisive positions of power in the Republican as well as in the Democratic party. But ironic or not, it is the case. For the first time in modern America a whole school of thought has consciously challenged the very foundations of collectivist Liberalism; two intellectually serious journals, *Modern Age* and *National Review,* have established themselves integrally in the life of the nation; and an increasing number of the newer generation of undergraduates, graduate students, and young instructors in the universities openly range themselves against the prevailing Liberal orthodoxy. Most important, perhaps, an intense and far-reaching discussion has been taking place among the enemies of Liberalism on the meaning and matter of their position in the circumstances of mid-twentieth-century America.

It is to this discussion that I want to address myself, with the hope of helping to clarify some of the issues which divide counsels and hinder the growth of intellectual understanding among the opponents of collectivism. Semantic difficulties are added to substantive difficulties in any such discussion, and I ask the indulgence of my readers in accepting the word "conservative" as an overall term to include the two streams of thought that in practice unite to oppose the reigning ideology of collectivist Liberalism. I believe that those two streams of thought, although they are sometimes presented as mutually incompatible, can in reality be united within a single broad conservative political theory, since they have their roots in a common tradition and are arrayed against a common enemy. Their opposition, which takes many forms, is essentially a division between those who abstract from the corpus of Western belief its stress upon freedom and upon the innate importance of the individual person (what we may call the "libertarian" position) and those who, drawing upon the same source, stress value and virtue and order (what we may call the "traditionalist" position).

But the source from which both draw, the continuing consciousness of Western civilization, has been specifically distinguished by its ability to hold these apparently opposed ends in balance and tension, and in fact the two positions which confront each other today in American conservative discourse both implicitly accept, to a large degree, the ends of the other. Without the implicit acceptance of an absolute ground of value, the preeminence of the person as criterion of political and social thought and action has no philosophical foundation, and freedom would be only a meaningless excitation and could never become the serious goal of a serious politics. On the other hand, the belief in virtue as the end of men's being implicitly recognizes the necessity of freedom to choose that end; otherwise, virtue could be no more than a conditioned tropism. And the raising of order to the rank of an end overshadowing and subordinating the individual person would make of order not what the traditionalist conservative means by it, but the rule of totalitarian authority, inhuman and subhuman.

On neither side is there a purposeful, philosophically founded rejection of the ends the other side proclaims. Rather, each side emphasizes so strongly the aspect of the great tradition of the West which it sees as decisive that distortion sets in. The place of its goals in the total tradition of the West is lost sight of, and the complementary interdependence of freedom and virtue, of the individual person and political order, is forgotten.

Nevertheless, although these contrary emphases in conservative thought can and do pull away from each other when the proponents of either forsake one side of their common heritage of belief in virtue as man's proper end *and* his freedom under God as the condition of the achievement of that end, their opposition is not irreconcilable, precisely because they do in fact jointly possess that very heritage. Extremists on one side may be undisturbed by the danger of the recrudescence of authoritarian status society if only it would enforce the doctrines in which they believe. Extremists on the other side may care little what becomes of ultimate values if only political and economic individualism prevails. But both extremes are self-defeating: truth withers when freedom dies, however righteous the authority that kills it; and free individualism uninformed by moral value rots at its core and soon brings about conditions that pave the way for surrender to tyranny.

Such extremes, however, are not the necessary outcome of a dialectic between doctrines which emphasize opposite sides of the same truth. Indeed, a dialectic between different emphases based upon the same fundamental understanding is the mode by which finite men have achieved much of the wisdom contained in tradition. Such a dialectic is in the highest degree necessary today between the libertarians and the traditionalists among conservatives. It cannot fail to achieve results of the greatest significance, if only the protagonists, in pressing that aspect of the truth which each regards as decisive, keep constantly in their consciousness other and complementary aspects of the same truth.

The tendency to establish false antitheses obstructing fruitful confrontation arises in part from an inherent dilemma of conservatism in a revolutionary era such as ours. There is a real contradiction between the deep piety of the conservative spirit towards tradition, prescription, the preservation of the fiber of society (what has been called "natural conservatism") and the more reasoned, consciously principled, militant conservatism which becomes necessary when the fibers of society have been rudely torn apart, when deleterious revolutionary principles ride high and restoration, not preservation, is the order of the day. For what the conservative is committed to conserve is not simply whatever happen to be the established conditions of a few years or a few decades, but the consensus of his civilization, of his country, as that consensus over the centuries has reflected truth derived from the very constitution of being. We are today historically in a situation created by thirty years of slow and insidious revolution at home and a half century of violent open revolution abroad. To conserve the true and the good under these circumstances is to restore an understanding (and a social structure reflecting that understanding) which has been all but buried; it is not to preserve the transient customs and prescriptions of the present.

It is here that the dilemma of conservatism affects our present doctrinal discussion. The need in our circumstances for the most vigorous use of reason to combat the collectivist, scientistic, amoral wave of the present tends to induce in the libertarian an apotheosis of reason and the neglect of tradition and prescription (which he identifies with the prevailing prescriptions of the present). The traditionalist, suspecting in this libertarian tendency the same fever to impose upon men an abstract speculative ideology that has characterized the revolution of our time—as well as the French Revolution and its spiritual forebears—tends to recoil and in his turn to press a one-sided position. Too often he confounds reason and principle with "demon ideology." Rather than justly insisting upon the limits of reason—the finite bounds of the purview of any one man or any one generation and the responsibility to employ reason in the context of continuing tradition—he seems sometimes to turn his back on reason altogether and to place the claims of custom and prescription in irreconcilable opposition to it.

Both attitudes obscure the truth; both vitiate the value of the dialectic. The history of the West has been a history of reason operating within tradition. The balance has been tenuous, the tension at times has tightened till it was spiritually almost unbearable; but out of this balance and tension the glory of the West has been created. To claim exclusive sovereignty for either component, reason or tradition, is to smirch that glory and cripple the potentialities of conservatism in its struggle against the Liberal-collectivist Leviathan.

Abstract reason, functioning in a vacuum of tradition, can indeed give birth to an arid and distorting ideology. But, in a revolutionary age, the qualities of natural conservatism by themselves can lead only to the enthronement of the prevailing power of the revolution. Natural conservatism is a legitimate human characteristic, and in settled times it is conducive to good. It represents the universal human tendency to hold by the accustomed, to maintain existing modes of life. In settled times it can exist in healthy tension with the other equally natural human characteristic, the dynamic impulse to break beyond accepted limits in the deepening of truth and the heightening of value. But this is only possible before the fibers of society have been loosened, before the "cake of custom" has been broken. Then these two human tendencies can be held in just proportion, since men of all conditions believe, each at the level of his understanding, in the same transcendent ground of truth and value. But when, through whatever cause, this unity in tension is riven, when the dynamic takes off into thin air, breaking its tension with the perpetual rhythms of life—in short, when a revolutionary force shatters the unity and balance of civilization—then conservatism must be of another sort if it is to fulfill its responsibility. It is not and cannot be limited to that uncritical acceptance, that uncomplicated reverence, which is the essence of natural conservatism. The world of idea and symbol and image has been turned topsy-turvy; the life stream of civilization has been cut off and dispersed.

This is our situation. What is required of us is a *conscious* conservatism, a clearly principled restatement in new circumstances of philosophical and political truth. This conscious conservatism cannot be a simple piety, although in a deep sense it must have piety towards the constitution of being. Nevertheless in its consciousness it necessarily reflects a reaction to the rude break the revolution has made in the continuity of human wisdom. It is called forth by a sense of the loss which that cutting off has created. It cannot now be identical with the natural conservatism towards which it yearns. The world in which it exists is the revolutionary world. To accept that, to conserve that, would be to accept and conserve the very denial of man's long-developed understanding, the very destruction of achieved truth, which are the essence of the revolution.

Nor can the conscious conservatism required of us appeal simply and uncomplicatedly to the past. The past has had many aspects, all held in measured suspension. But the revolution has destroyed that suspension, that tradition; the delicate fabric can never be re-created in the identical form; its integral character has been destroyed. The conscious conservatism of a revolutionary or postrevolutionary era faces problems inconceivable to the natural conservatism of a prerevolutionary time. The modes of thought of natural conservatism are not by themselves adequate to the tasks of a time like this. Today's conservatism cannot simply affirm. It must select and adjudge. It is conservative because in its selection and in its judgment it bases itself upon the accumulated wisdom of mankind over millennia, because it accepts the limits upon the irresponsible play of untrammeled reason which the unchanging values exhibited by that wisdom dictate. But it is, it has to be, not acceptance of what lies before it in the contemporary world, but challenge. In an era like ours the existing regime in philosophical thought, as in political and social actuality, is fundamentally wrong. To accept is to be not conservative but acquiescent to revolution.

Situations of this nature have arisen again and again in the history of civilization, and each time the great renewers have been those who were able to recover true principle out of the wreck of their heritage. They were guided by reason—reason mediated, it is true, by prudence, but in the first instance reason. Like Socrates, Plato, Aristotle, confronting the chaos in the body politic and in the minds of men created by the overweening pride of the Athenian *demos,* we do not live in the happy age of a natural conservatism. We cannot simply revere; we cannot uncritically follow tradition, for the tradition presented to us is rapidly becoming—thanks to the prevailing intellectual climate, thanks to the schools, thanks to the outpourings of all the agencies that mould opinion and belief—the tradition of a positivism scornful of truth and virtue, the tradition of the collective, the tradition of the untrammeled state.

The conservative today, like the conscious conservative of all revolutionary eras, cannot escape the necessity and the duty to bring reason to bear upon the problems that confront him. He has to separate the true from the false, applying basic principle to the task of cutting through the tangled mass of confusion and falsehood; he has the responsibility of establishing in new circumstances forms of thought and institutional arrangements which will express the truth of the great tradition of the West. Respectful though he is of the wisdom of the past and reverent towards precedent and prescription, the tasks he faces can only be carried out with the aid of reason, the faculty which enables us to distinguish principle and thus to separate the true from the false.

The projection of a sharp antithesis between reason and tradition distorts the true harmony that exists between them and blocks the development of conservative thought. There is no real antagonism. Conservatism to continue to develop today must embrace both: reason operating within tradition; neither ideological *hubris* abstractly creating Utopian blueprints, ignoring the accumulated wisdom of mankind, nor blind depen-

dence upon that wisdom to answer automatically the questions
posed to our generation and demanding our own expenditure
of our mind and spirit.

Closely related to the false antithesis between reason and tradition that distorts the dialogue between the libertarian emphasis and the traditionalist emphasis among conservatives is
our historical inheritance of the nineteenth-century European
struggle between classical liberalism and a conservatism that
was too often rigidly authoritarian. Granted there is much in
classical liberalism that conservatives must reject—its philosophical foundations, its tendency towards Utopian constructions, its disregard (explicitly, though by no means implicitly)
of tradition—and granted it is the source of much that is responsible for the plight of the twentieth century, its championship of freedom and its development of political and economic
theories directed towards the assurance of freedom have contributed to our heritage concepts which we need to conserve
and develop, as surely as we need to reject the utilitarian ethics
and the secular progressivism that classical liberalism has also
passed on to us.

Nineteenth-century conservatism, with all its understanding
of the preeminence of virtue and value, for all its piety towards
the continuing tradition of mankind, was far too cavalier to the
claims of freedom, far too ready to subordinate the individual
person to the authority of state or society.

The conservative today is the inheritor of the best in both
these tragically bifurcated branches of the Western tradition,
but the division lingers on and adds to the difficulties of conservative discourse. The traditionalist, although in practice he
fights alongside the libertarian against the collectivist Leviathan state of the twentieth century, tends to reject the political
and economic theories of freedom which flow from classical
liberalism in his reaction against its unsound metaphysics. He
discards the true with the false, creating unnecessary obstacles

to the mutual dialogue in which he is engaged with his libertarian *alter ego*. The libertarian, suffering from the mixed heritage of the nineteenth-century champions of liberty, reacts against the traditionalist's emphasis upon precedent and continuity out of antipathy to the authoritarianism with which that emphasis has been associated, although in actuality he stands firmly for continuity and tradition against the rising revolutionary wave of collectivism and statism.

We are victims here of an inherent tragedy in the history of classical liberalism. As it developed the economic and political doctrines of limited state power, the free-market economy, and the freedom of the individual person, it sapped, by its utilitarianism, the foundations of belief in an organic moral order. But the only possible basis of respect for the integrity of the individual person and for the overriding value of his freedom is belief in an organic moral order. Without such a belief, no doctrine of political and economic liberty can stand.

Furthermore, when such a belief is not universally accepted, a free society, even if it could exist, would become licentious war of all against all. Political freedom, failing a broad acceptance of the personal obligation to duty and to charity, is never viable. Deprived of an understanding of the philosophical foundations of freedom and exposed to the ravening of conscienceless marauders, men forget that they are fully men only to the degree that they are free to choose their destiny, and they turn to whatever fallacy promises them welfare and order.

The classical liberal as philosopher dug away the foundations of the economic and political doctrines of classical liberalism. But however much he may thereby have contributed to our misfortunes, he himself continued to live on the inherited moral capital of centuries of Christendom. His philosophical doctrines attacked the foundations of conscience, but he himself was still a man of conscience. As Christopher Dawson has said: "The old liberalism, with all its shortcoming, had its roots deep in the soul of Western and Christian culture." With those

roots as yet unsevered, the classical liberal was able to develop
the theories of political and economic freedom which are part
of the conservative heritage today.

The misunderstanding between libertarian and traditionalist
are to a considerable degree the result of a failure to understand the differing levels on which classical liberal doctrines
are valid and invalid. Although the classical liberal forgot—and
the contemporary libertarian conservative sometimes tends to
forget—that in the *moral* realm freedom is only a means
whereby men can pursue their proper end, which is virtue, he
did understand that in the *political* realm freedom is the primary end. If, with Acton, we "take the establishment of liberty
for the realization of moral duties to be the end of civil society," the traditionalist conservative of today, living in an age
when liberty is the last thought of our political mentors, has
little cause to reject the contributions to the understanding of
liberty of the classical liberals, however corrupted their understanding of the ends of liberty. Their error lay largely in the
confusion of the temporal with the transcendent. They could
not distinguish between the *authoritarianism* with which men
and institutions suppress the freedom of men and the *authority*
of God and truth.

On the other hand, the same error in reverse vitiated the
thought of nineteenth-century conservatives. They respected
the authority of God and of truth as conveyed in tradition, but
too often they imbued the authoritarianism of men and institutions with the sacred aura of divine authority. They gave way to
the temptation to make of tradition, which in its rightful role
serves as a guide to the operation of reason, a weapon with
which to suppress reason.

It is true that from their understanding of the basis of men's
moral existence, from their reverence for the continuity and
precedent that tie the present to the past, contemporary conservatism has inherited elements vital to its very existence. Yet

we can no more make of the great conservative minds of the
nineteenth century unerring guides to be blindly followed
than we can condemn out of hand their classical liberal opponents. Sound though they were on the essentials of man's being, on his destiny to virtue and his responsibility to seek it, on
his duty in the moral order, they failed too often to realize that
the *political* condition of moral fulfillment is freedom from coercion. Signally they failed to recognize the decisive danger in
a union of political and economic power, a danger becoming
daily greater before their eyes as science and technology created apace immense aggregates of economic energy. Aware, as
the classical liberals were not, of the reality of original sin, they
forgot that its effects are never more virulent than when men
wield unlimited power. Looking to the state to promote virtue,
they forgot that the power of the state rests in the hands of
men as subject to the effects of original sin as those they govern. They could not, or would not, see a truth the classical liberals understood: if to the power naturally inherent in the
state, to defend its citizens from violence, domestic and foreign, and to administer justice, there is added a positive power
over economic and social energy, the temptation to tyranny becomes irresistible, and the political conditions of freedom
wither.

The tendency of the traditionalist conservative to insist that
the crystallization of a conservative outlook today requires only
that we carry on the principles of those who called themselves
conservatives in the nineteenth century oversimplifies and
confuses the problem. That the conservative is one who preserves tradition does not mean that his task is arid imitation
and repetition of what others have done before. Certainly in
ultimate terms, upon the basic issue of human destiny, truths
have been given us that we cannot improve upon, that we can
only convey and make real in the context of our time. Here
indeed the conservatives of the nineteenth century played a
heroic part in preserving in the teeth of the overwhelming ten-

dency of the era the age-old image of man as a creature of transcendent destiny.

In the political and economic realm, however, these truths establish only the foundation for an understanding of the end of civil society and the function of the state. That end, to guarantee freedom, so that men may uncoercedly pursue virtue, can be achieved in different circumstances by different means. To the clarification of what these means are in specific circumstances, the conservative must apply his reason. The technological circumstances of the twentieth century demand above all the breaking up of power and the separation of centers of power within the economy itself, within the state itself, and between the state and the economy. Power of a magnitude never before dreamed of by men has been brought into being. While separation of power has always been essential to a good society, if those who possess it are to be preserved from corruption and those who do not are to be safeguarded from coercion, this has become a fateful necessity under the conditions of modern technology. To the analysis of this decisive problem and to the development of political and economic solutions of it, classical liberalism contributed mightily. If we reject that heritage, we should be casting away some of the most powerful among our weapons against socialism, Communism, and collectivist Liberalism. The traditionalist who would have us do so because of the philosophical errors of classical liberalism, like the libertarian who rejects tradition because it has sometimes been associated with authoritarianism, seriously weakens the development of conservative doctrine.

The historical fact is—and it adds to the complexity of our problems—that the great tradition of the West has come to us through the nineteenth century, split, bifurcated, so that we must draw not only upon those who called themselves conservatives in that century but also upon those who called themselves liberals. The economists of the liberal British tradition, from Adam Smith through and beyond the vilified Manchesterians, like the Austrian economists from Menger and Böhm-Bawerk to Mises and Hayek, analyzed the conditions of industrial society and established the principles upon which the colossal power that it produces can be developed for the use of man without nurturing a monstrous Leviathan. Without their mighty intellectual endeavor, we should be disarmed before the collectivist economics of Marx, Keynes, and Galbraith. And in the sphere of political theory, who has surpassed the nineteenth-century liberals in their prophetic understanding of the looming dangers of the all-powerful state? Conservatives today can reject neither side of their nineteenth-century heritage; they must draw upon both.

Differences of emphasis between libertarian and traditionalist cannot be avoided and should not be regretted. Conservatism has no monolithic party line. Our task is to overcome the nineteenth-century bifurcation of the Western tradition in fruitful dialogue, not to perpetuate it by refusing to understand the breadth and complexity of our heritage, out of a narrow historicism that unearths outworn party emblems.

I am well aware that what I have been saying can be criticized as eclecticism and attacked as an effort to smother principle. But it is not the laying aside of clear belief, either by the libertarian conservative or by the traditionalist conservative, in order to present a front against contemporary collectivist Liberalism, that is here conceived. Rather it is the deepening of the beliefs which each holds through the development of their implications in a dialectic free of distorting narrowness. That deepening—and the development of a common conservative doctrine, comprehending both emphases—cannot be achieved in a surface manner by blinking differences or blurring intellectual distinctions with grandiose phraseology. It can be achieved only by a hard-fought dialectic—a dialectic in which both sides recognize not only that they have a common enemy but also that, despite all differences, they hold a common heritage.

As Americans, indeed, we have a great tradition to draw upon, in which the division, the bifurcation, of European thought between the emphasis on virtue and value and order and the emphasis on freedom and the integrity of the individual person was overcome, and a harmonious unity of the tensed poles of Western thought was achieved in political theory and practice as never before or since. The men who created the Republic, who framed the Constitution and produced that monument of political wisdom, *The Federalist Papers,* comprised among them as great a conflict of emphasis as any in contemporary American conservatism. Washington, Franklin, Jefferson, Hamilton, Adams, Jay, Mason, Madison—among them there existed immense differences on the claims of the individual person and the claims of order, on the relation of virtue to freedom. But their dialectic was conducted within a continuing awareness of their joint heritage. Out of that dialectic they created a political theory and a political structure based upon the understanding that, while truth and virtue are metaphysical and moral ends, the freedom to seek them is the political condition of those ends—and that a social structure which keeps power divided is the indispensable means to this political end. The debate from which our American institutions arose is a fitting model for our debate.

That debate will the more rapidly and the more profoundly develop the energy and the fruitfulness and the eventual understanding that are intellectually inherent in the opposed emphases, if we constantly keep in mind the vision of life against which we are jointly engaged in fateful combat: the Liberal-collectivist body of dogma that has pervaded the consciousness and shaped the actions of the decisive and articulate sections of society over the past half century or more.

In opposition to this image of man as neither free nor inspired by a transcendent destiny, the differences between libertarian and traditionalist are thrown into their true perspective: differences of emphasis, not of underlying opposition. In the light of this, libertarian and traditionalist, as they deepen their understanding in a commonly based dialogue, can maintain a common front and a common struggle. The desecration of the image of man, the attack alike upon his freedom and his transcendent dignity, provide common cause in the immediate struggle. As with our ancestors who laid the foundations of the Republic, the challenge to our common faith inspires us, without surrendering our differences of stress, to create a fundamental unity of doctrine within which libertarian and traditionalist, respecting each other, can mutually vindicate the true nature of man, free and responsible, against the arid, mechanistic, collectivist denial of man's nature which transitorily prevails.

PART TWO

IN DEFENSE
OF FREEDOM
A Conservative
Credo

1

FREEDOM AND
CONSERVATISM

My intention in writing this book is to vindicate the
freedom of the person as the central and primary
end of political society. I am also concerned with
demonstrating the integral relationship between freedom as a
political end and the basic beliefs of contemporary American
conservatism.

Liberalism was indeed once, in the last century, the proponent and defender of freedom. But that which is called liberalism today has deserted its heritage of defense of the freedom
of the person to become the peculiarly American form of what
in Europe is called democratic socialism. This transformation
was the result of a fatal flaw in the philosophical underpin-
nings of nineteenth-century liberalism. It stood for individual
freedom, but its utilitarian philosophical attitude denied the
validity of moral ends firmly based on the constitution of being. Thereby, with this denial of an ultimate sanction for the
inviolability of the person, liberalism destroyed the very foundations of its defense of the person as primary in political and
social matters.

The complex story of the actual transformation of liberalism—a transformation unfolding out of this profound original

Reprinted from *In Defense of Freedom: A Conservative Credo* (Chicago: Henry
Regnery, 1962), by permission.

defect—is a fascinating chapter in intellectual history. That is not, however, the subject of this book. Although I shall touch upon it from time to time, my concern here is not with the history of liberalism but with what is today called liberalism—alike by those who are hostile to it and by those who consciously write and act as "liberals." This usage is the only meaning the word retains in common discourse. Therefore, to distinguish contemporary "liberalism" from the liberalism of the nineteenth century—and in piety towards the nineteenth-century liberals to whom the freedom of the person was a dear concern—I shall throughout this book refer to what is today called liberalism as collectivist liberalism.

If, however, nineteenth-century liberalism by its fundamental philosophical errors gave birth to that form of twentieth-century collectivism which passes under the name of liberalism, there was in nineteenth-century conservatism an inherent flaw of another sort. The conservatives of the last century were sound in their fundamental philosophical position, upholding the objective existence of values based upon the unchanging constitution of being as the criterion for moral thought and action. They staunchly held the line against the assault of utilitarianism, positivism, and scientism; but on another level they failed philosophically, deeply misreading the nature of man. They would not or they could not see the correlative to their fundamental philosophical position: acceptance of the moral authority derived from transcendent criteria of truth and good must be voluntary if it is to have meaning; if it is coerced by human force, it is meaningless. They were willing, if only the right standards were upheld, to accept an authoritarian structure of state and society. They were, at the best, indifferent to freedom in the body politic; at the worst, its enemies.

There are in the contemporary American scene those who take their inspiration from these nineteenth-century conservative beliefs. Although they do not compose an organized political group (some of them, indeed, in their practical political influence are essentially part of the "liberal" establishment, while others are allied with the American conservative movement), they do hold a common theoretical position. This position is generally described as the New Conservatism. Although that phrase is sometimes also used more broadly to refer to the whole contemporary American conservative movement, it is in the specific and limited sense that I shall employ it in this book.

The concepts on which the New Conservatives base themselves can be directly traced to nineteenth-century conservatism and to certain aspects of the thinking of Edmund Burke, who is explicitly recognized by most of them as a major source of their guiding ideas. Their position is characterized by an organic view of society, by a subordination of the individual person to society, and, therefore, by a denial that the freedom of the person is the decisive criterion of a good polity.

This subordination of freedom, this exaltation of the claims of society, differentiates them from the implicit consensus of contemporary American conservatism. That consensus, it is true, does agree with the New Conservatives on the moral obligation of all men to seek and to respect the norms of virtue objectively based upon an eternal order of truth and good; but in contradistinction to them, it posits as a necessary corollary that the freedom of the person, not the asserted authority of "society," of some "mysterious incorporation of the human race," is primary in political thought and action.

Should the question be raised, by what right do I maintain against the New Conservatives and the other heirs of nineteenth-century conservatism that the position which I am defending is essentially the consensus of contemporary American conservatism, I point first to the empirical evidence—and on several levels. At the source to which American conservatism inevitably returns—the Declaration of Independence, the Constitution, and the debates at the time of its adoption—this simultaneous belief in objectively existing moral value and in the freedom of the individual person was promulgated in uncompromising terms. From that source it irradiates the active present scene of American conservatism. The broadly acknowledged political symbol of American conservatism, Barry Goldwater, and its broadly acknowledged intellectual spokesman, William F. Buckley, Jr., share this twin belief. As M. Stanton Evans, in *Revolt on the Campus*,[1] has shown in copious quotations from the leaders of the conservative student movement, it is their guiding light. What is true of the young is also true of the great majority of adult conservatives. A serious examination of the publications of the various groups among conservatives will, I am convinced, prove this contention to the disinterested reader.

The position taken in this book is, I believe, an accurate representation, a crystallization on the theoretical level, of the empirical attitudes of the widespread and developing American conservative movement. But this very combination of freedom and moral authority—which in the ideological history of the European nineteenth century were the symbols of opposed liberal and conservative forces—has been the target of sharp theoretical attack by collectivist-liberal writers and even by some conservatives of the nineteenth-century tradition. We are told that what is not in the tradition of Burke—or of the medieval synthesis—or of Plato—cannot call itself conservatism: anyone who insists upon freedom in the political and economic sphere together with "legitimate" conservative beliefs is really half liberal, half conservative, a sad case of intellectual schizophrenia. Such criticisms might be answered by simply pointing to actuality, asserting that, whether European intellectual history blesses us or not, this is the way the average contemporary American conservative thinks and feels; or by citing the founding documents of the Republic as authority—the authority of another, an American, intellectual history.

---

1. M. Stanton Evans, *Revolt on the Campus* (Chicago: Henry Regnery, 1961), 180–85.

But, in candor, this is not enough. It has to be shown that the two aspects of the position are fundamentally in accord, that they are grounded both in the nature of men and in the very constitution of being. It is my aim to make this demonstration, to vindicate on theoretical grounds the native belief of American conservatives that freedom as a prime criterion in the political and social sphere is not alien to the conservative view of man's nature and destiny, that it arises naturally from conservative assumptions, and that it can be effectively defended only upon the basis of those assumptions.

Therefore, the concern of these pages is with establishing the theoretical soundness of this position. I am not primarily concerned with the details or the limitations of present-day political reality, but rather with developing a conservative criterion for a good society, a good polity. That being my intent, the standard of judgment of political questions here presented is just that: a standard, not a program for immediate achievement. I would add, however, that without something in the nature of an ideal image of what a good society should be, without an end which political action can strive to approximate, there is no basis for judging the rights and wrongs of the practical alternatives that constantly present themselves.

The specific character of the concrete political forms indicated by this criterion for any given society will vary immensely depending on the civilizational development and the experience with free institutions of the nation or culture concerned. In the United States, with our Constitutional tradition and Constitutional experience, a comparatively close approximation to the ideal is possible, despite the attrition of several decades of liberal-collectivist ascendancy. For ours is the most effective effort ever made to articulate in *political* terms the Western understanding of the interrelation of the freedom of the person and the authority of an objective moral order. The other nations of Western civilization—all respecters of the person, but without the rock-bound theory of limited government that inspired the American Founders—hold, in varying degree, the preeminence of the person in their tradition; therefore they approximate, if less closely, to the political ideal here presented. The tradition of the Oriental and Middle Eastern civilizations is still further removed from it; and precivilized cultures, such as those of Africa, are at an enormous remove from it.

I realize that such a ranking of nations and cultures, particularly one which places one's own country at the head, will be regarded in the relativist atmosphere of the day as extraordinarily unenlightened and arrogant. Be that as it may, by the criterion I hope to establish, it is the truth; and it is therefore primarily to the United States and secondarily to Western civilization that my analysis has direct relevance.

Furthermore, I should add, lest specious conclusions be drawn from the defense of the freedom of the person, that there is here no advocacy of that equalitarianism which would forbid to men the acquisition of unequal goods, influence, or honor and the right to pass these "inequalities" on to their heirs if they can. The only equality that can be legitimately derived from the premises of the freedom of the person is the equal right of all men to be free from coercion exercised against their life, liberty, and property. This is the touchstone of a free society. For the rest, the capabilities of men, specific and inherited, should determine their position, their influence, and the respect in which they are held.

Nor does it follow from my thesis that any particular type of political institution is in itself either demanded by, or a guarantee of, development towards a free society. The representative democratic institutions combined with constitutional guarantees of freedom, which have been the matrix for the development of free societies in the United States, England, and some other Western nations, may not be the best political forms for the achievement of an approximation to a good society even in all countries of Western civilization, much less elsewhere.

But, although there is more than one possible form of political institution for the development of a good society, there are also forms which are totally negative to any such development. Nazism, which was inspired by the concept of reducing the person to nothingness before the state, was destroyed in the war of 1939–45; but Communism, its older brother, today dominates a third of the world and advances with messianic zeal and cold scientific strategy towards the domination of the whole world. Consequently, everything projected in this book presupposes the defeat of this monstrous, atavistic attack upon the survival of the very concepts of moral order and individual freedom. If I do not deal with Communism, it is because I am here concerned with the development of ideas within the Western and American tradition. With Communism, which bases itself on a set of values radically hostile in their very foundation to the Western view of man, there is no common ground for theoretical discussion. Determination and force will decide the issue, and our determination and force—which can be expressed only in terms of counterattack—will depend upon the depth with which we understand and, understanding, are loyal to the truths incarnate in Western civilization and the American republic.

To the drawing out and clarification of these truths, this book is dedicated. In that effort, my central endeavor is to validate the individual person as the decisive concern of political action and political theory. The individual person and social institutions are the polar points to which every political philosophy is oriented. And as men's political arrangements reflect their consciousness, it is by the emphasis placed upon one or the other of these poles by the prevalent political philosophy that the characteristics of a political society are established and perpetuated.

It is my general contention that, despite the weight of the tradition of our civilization on the side of the individual person, the predominant intellectual tendency of this century has brought about a deep derangement of the tension between these two poles of human existence, towards the submergence of the person. It is my particular contention that the criticism by the New Conservatives of this prevailing collectivist dogma itself suffers from an inner error of political understanding.

Against both the prevailing mode of thought and the New Conservative criticism, which are, each in its own way, appeals to experience, I propose the claims of reason and the claims of the tradition of reason. I do not assume that reason is the sole possession of a single living generation, or of any man in any generation. I do assume that it is the active quality whereby men (starting with a due respect for the fundamental moral knowledge of ends and values incorporated in tradition) have the power to distinguish what ought to be from what is, the ideal from the dictates of power. Upon these assumptions, I shall attempt to reestablish, in contemporary contexts, principles drawn from the nature of man and by these principles to criticize both the prevalent collectivist-liberal orthodoxy and the New Conservatism.

Both, I hope to show, share in political matters a common error which brings them much closer together than the polemics exchanged between them would seem to indicate. Both are radically affected by the derangement of the tension between the person and social institutions necessary to a good society. Both give so high a place to the concept of society that the freedom of the person is reduced to a subordinate position and becomes transformed from a real end into a pious hope—invoked on suitable occasions but to be achieved as the implicit result of the establishment of the "right" social pattern, not to be striven for directly. Both reduce the person to a secondary being, whose dignity and rights become dependent upon the gift and grace of society or the state.

2

CLEARING GROUND

It is impossible to come to grips with the problem of freedom and with the interrelated problem of the individual and society without first clearing some ground. Before the questions themselves can be fruitfully discussed, it is necessary to say something about the way in which we have become accustomed to think and speak of them, about what is now the generally accepted method of political and social thought. That method not only affects fundamental enquiry concerning political and social matters; it also affects our efforts to handle the practical and immediate political situations which press upon us. Our inability to act confidently in the face of upsetting phenomena as divergent as our successive defeats by the Soviet Union in the world arena or the growth of juvenile delinquency has its roots in a fundamental derangement of our way of thinking about the world. We concentrate upon problems that seem to multiply hydralike, rather than upon the principles that bear upon the problems; and this creates the suffocating verbiage of so much contemporary political and social discussion. Like a bevy of old wives congregated about the bedside of a suffering patient, every pundit presses his own nostrum, each directed towards a conspicuous symptom; and, as the chatter arises, it drowns the voice and crazes the mind of anyone attempting to assess the underlying malady which creates the symptoms.

Worse, in the prevailing intellectual atmosphere the very

concept of a theoretical enquiry into political and social matters which is based upon a moral or philosophical value system
and developed in terms of the nature of man is the subject of
scorn. By a misleading analogy with physical science—where
the objects of study are but objects, without subjectivity, will,
conscious self-direction—social theory becomes "the social sciences" and political theory becomes "political science," disciplines conceived in slavish imitation of the natural sciences. An
entire dimension is exiled from consideration, a dimension
which in the natural sciences does not and could not exist: the
dimension of the ideal, of the end and direction of action, of
what ought to be. But the great tradition of Western thought,
which gave form to the political concepts and institutions we
have inherited, found in the tension between what ought to be
and what is the beginning and the continuing center of political theory. However different their approach, however different their practical conclusions, this is as true of Dante as of
Aquinas, of the Puritan republicans as of the Stuart apologists
for the divine right of kings. And, although by the eighteenth
century the corrosive influence of scientism had already begun
to eat away at the theoretical foundations of political thought,
it remained as true of Adams as of Jefferson, of Calhoun as of
Lincoln.

Scientism and the Study of Politics

Just where and how the other conception, the scientistic conception, the idea that the study of politics is a science in the
same sense and with the same methods as the study of natural
phenomena, became a central theme and dominant mode of
social scholarship is a fascinating and depressing study, but one
which it would be impossible to develop within the limits of
this book. Suffice it to say that today the learned authority
upon politics is either the *Realpolitiker,* the political tough guy

who advises those with power how to use it in order to get more power, or the expert on the interview and the statistic, the indefatigable pollster whose idea of political study is to register the impulses of the uninformed and uninstructed mass. The former considers political thought a "policy science"; the latter, a "behavioral science." But they are in agreement that political science is limited to an analysis of what is, that it has no relationship to moral or philosophical enquiry. This attitude, the influence of which has spread far beyond the confines of scholarship, permeating the outlook of journalist, telecaster, and politician, draws its underlying assumptions from the empirical and naturalistic position of Machiavelli and Hobbes. These assumptions have been immensely reinforced in the past hundred years by the prestige the natural sciences and their methods have acquired.

It is here that the prevailing doctrines go astray. The sphere of natural studies contains no element of consciousness with its innate corollary of freedom and moral responsibility. But any study that aspires to throw light upon man must take account of these autonomous aspects of his being. It is possible to study the proton, the meson, the electron, without any consideration of their inner being or of consciousness. Even with nonhuman life—that intermediate mode of being between the inorganic and the human—there is no way of knowing, language lacking, the degree or level of consciousness. While, by analogy, we may justly attribute a nearer approach to consciousness to animals than to the inorganic world, we still have no forcing knowledge that denies us the right to learn what we can solely by external consideration of their behavior.

A methodology which is richly rewarding when it deals with the "how" of inorganic processes and which has moderate results insofar as it considers the lower forms of life can be applied to human beings only by a perversion of the principle of analogy. To do so is deliberately to put blinkers upon our eyes, to refuse to consider the material available to our judgments.

The principle of analogy functions validly when, from things we know much about, we derive insights into things about which our information is limited. But to insist that methods which seem valid for the study of fields where consciousness is not involved will bring fruitful results when applied to the study of human beings, who are endowed with consciousness, a study where we are richly provided with direct knowledge of consciousness—this is to transform the principle of analogy into its opposite. It is to move from solid forms to images. Where we have direct knowledge, we do not need analogy. The validity of a method applicable where our information can only be from the outside arises from the fact that it is the best method we have. It is absurd to use such a method in an area where our knowledge from the inside is so rich as to be often-times embarrassing.

Any "science" of man which pretends to a fruitful utilization of the methods and techniques of the natural sciences does so and can do so only by ignoring an enormous and decisive aspect of the actuality of men. For men's knowledge of themselves is first of all direct: that which they know of their own consciousness from their own consciousness. To attempt to arrive at an understanding of men indirectly, by an examination of their actions, their "behavior," is to arrive only at knowledge of a truncated mechanical model which resembles man only in externals.

It should be remarked in passing that to reject the validity of the scientific methodology for the study of man is not to deny the usefulness of that methodology in auxiliary studies which are secondarily relevant to the study of man. Even here, however, there is a limitation. Analytical and statistical studies of such problems as population, employment, the geographical distribution of voting trends, can throw light upon the study of man; but they are only reliable under the condition that they measure activities undertaken quite independently of the observer. That is, when a man votes in an election or purchases a commodity on the market, an act has taken place, and it is subject to the same kind of objective observation as the motion of a physical body; but when a sociologist or a "political scientist" asks a set of questions whose sole function is to serve his research, questions in which the man interviewed has no stake, the scientific character is largely vitiated. The results must be judged much as the results achieved by a student of the same process, with no pretensions to the scientific method, would be judged; in both cases the results reflect the understanding and insight of the student of the problem. The quasi-scientific trimmings detract, if anything, from the validity of the findings, for a painful effort of analysis is necessary to discover whatever truths of insight lie behind the statistical findings. In view of the nonindependent character of the questions, the answers can reflect little more than the value system and the judgment of those who constructed them.

Scientific method, in a word, is valid for the study of man only when it is possible to study unaffected behavior objectively; and its value is limited and auxiliary, because the conclusions achieved will not be knowledge *of* men, but simply knowledge of some aspects of their behavior. Only when it is assumed, in sycophantic imitation of the natural sciences, that there is no valid knowledge except knowledge of that which can be objectively observed, manipulated, and measured, can the study of behavior be substituted for the study of man and glorified as the only possible form of the study of man.

The Appeal from Marx to Freud

In recent years, it is true, the poverty of the results achieved by the accepted methods has impelled a turn among social scientists from total concentration upon behavioral social processes towards grudging consideration of the possible significance of individuality. But so divorced have contemporary scholars become from the broader philosophical tradition, and so concerned are the social scientists lest they move outside the methodology of the natural sciences, that the individual person with whom they pretend to deal turns out to have a curious identity with the robot of the social behaviorism they began by criticizing. Between the views of W. H. MacDougall or George H. Mead and those of Clyde Kluckhohn or Margaret Mead, the essential difference is very slight indeed.

The appeal now is to Freud, but not to the dynamic Freud who, when deterministic scientism had deprived man of soul and free will, at least gave him back an autonomous biological constitution and a free "id." Rather it takes from psychoanalysis—preferably from the watered-down socialized neo-Freudianism of Sullivan, Fromm, and Horney—a set of descriptive terms with which it proceeds to construct its "models" of man, "models" distinguished from the earlier models of the social determinists only as Detroit generally distinguishes this year's model from last year's—by a somewhat different and, for the moment, more fashionable placing of the chrome.

Looking back upon the earlier trend of sociology with its tremendous debt to Marx and contrasting it with what they fondly describe as a new "turn," from emphasis upon "man in general [to] the individual person," two eminent sociologists of the new dispensation write: "If Marx stratified man, then Freud individualized him. Marxian theory focused our attention upon the coercive role of culture and stressed the process of social change. Freudian theory illuminated the behavior of individual personalities subjected to this cultural patterning and stressed the process of social adjustment."[2]

This would seem to say that Marx (and with him the main

2. Ernest R. Hilgard and Daniel Lerner, "The Person: Subject and Object of Science and Policy," in *The Policy Sciences,* ed. Daniel Lerner and Harold D. Lasswell (Stanford: Stanford University Press, 1951), 17.

twentieth-century trend in the social sciences) concentrated our attention upon society's role as omnipotent creator and controller of the person, while Freud concentrated it upon the way in which the person is created and controlled by society. This interpretation of Freud is no more a charter for the individual than are the theories of Marx. And indeed the writers go on to say, in an incredible contradiction which shows how alien to their minds is the concept of freedom: "Freud set man free . . . Freud set man afloat in an interpersonal universe by making untenable [the] historic conception of man as a rational, volitional, autonomous individual."[3]

The Autonomy of Man

Neither to the older nor to the newer forms of the scientistic methodology will this book make any concessions. Its fundamental premise *is* the "historic conception of man as a rational, volitional, autonomous individual," as a free being who lives between good and evil, beauty and ugliness, truth and error, and fulfills his destiny in the choices he makes.

This power to make choices, this innate freedom lies at the center of the drama of human existence. It is given immediately to every man's consciousness as a primary datum, along with his awareness of "the other," the externally determined, the objective world. Indeed, in mutual opposition, the self and "the other," the subjective and the objective, define each other and together exhaustively constitute the primitive content of consciousness. No objective methodology, however strict, can disprove the existence of the autonomous self and validate determinism, as no intuitive outlook, based upon the subjective, can disprove the existence of the external world and validate solipsism.

3. Ibid.

The "interpersonal" universe, like the universe of the behaviorists or the cultural relativists, rests upon data derived from apprehension of the external world. But that apprehension is no stronger than its twin apprehension: apprehension of the subjective, of the autonomy of the person. Therefore, no system built upon the one apprehension can logically deny the validity of the other without denying its own validity. To the degree that a fundamental premise systematically neglects either side of the tension between self and nonself, which is the only ground from which human thought can in reality proceed, it must perforce limp one-leggedly behind the full capacities of human understanding.

Primary Assumptions

The apprehension of man as of such a nature that innate freedom is of the essence of his being, is the central axiom upon which this critique of political thought is founded. It further assumes that the primary mode of achieving understanding in the study of man, more particularly in moral and political enquiry, is the use of reason operating within and upon tradition, reason deriving extended conclusions from simple apprehensions of the nature of man. Man as he exists, a complex whole, is the starting point. The conclusions are the principles which define the social and political conditions under which he can best fulfill his innate destiny.

They are, indeed, ideal principles and must be adapted in the light of the material situation and the demands of conflicting interests. They will need to be made concrete in different ways under different circumstances. But, although the ideal conclusions of political theory are not programmatic directives for detailed political action, this in no way negates the role and necessity of political theory. To bring about an approximation in actuality to an ideal set of limiting conditions is, or should be, the function of the art of politics, not the function of political theory. To think otherwise would be Utopian, to conceive once more of men as manipulable particles subject to the forming activity of the social engineer. The art of politics at its best is guided by fundamental principle, but operates by judgment, by prudence. Both are necessary; without the guiding principles of political theory, based in turn upon fundamental philosophical considerations, the practical art of politics is without direction and soon becomes an exercise in expediency for expediency's sake.

3

WHY FREEDOM?

To the primary proposition that innate freedom is an essential aspect of man's being, I join another proposition of a more specifically political character: that social and political organization, however important as a condition of existence, is, like oxygen or water, a condition, not the end, of the life of the individual person. At the best, proper social and political circumstances, like a rich and well-tilled seedbed, can provide felicitous circumstances in which a man may work out his fortune or misfortune, his good or ill. At the worst, they may cramp the field of his existence to a compass scarcely recognizable as human, although even then they cannot destroy the self-determination of his inner spiritual life. But, at best or worse, the social and political situation remains a situation more or less conducive to the worthy consummation of each man's drama, not a determining factor of it.

In one period of happier circumstance, Oliver Goldsmith and Dr. Johnson wrote:

> How small, of all that human hearts endure,
> That part which kings or laws can cause or cure!

The joint development of modern science and totalitarianism has increased the evil that state power can cause, but there is still a very small part of that which "human hearts endure" that the state can alleviate. So far as the increased power of the state to bring evil to the individual is concerned, that power is directly proportional to the pretences the state makes to control men's lives for good. To the degree that the political theory upon which the state is founded regards political and social institutions not simply as a condition of human existence, but as the determining cause of the well-being of men, the more it becomes an active source of ill-being. This much one can concede as a twentieth-century gloss on the eighteenth-century couplet: the state can cause greater harm than then, but cure no more.

Society Not a Real Entity

That which is not a determining cause but merely a condition cannot be considered independently as a true end; it must be considered in subordination to that of which it is a condition. Society and the state were made for individual men, not men for them. This was once a truism in America and through much of the West; but in the past few decades all the prospering political ideologies—Communism and Nazism, socialism, the milder theories of the welfare state—have founded themselves upon the opposite axiom, that individual men are secondary to society.

True, all these societal views proclaim—Communists no less than the social worker servitors of the welfare state—that they are directed towards the welfare of men, or at least towards the greatest welfare of the greatest number of men. But in all of them, the ground of the value judgments upon which every crucial decision is based is the abstract construct, society. None of them ever takes the person—not in mass, not in grouped "minorities," but in his single majesty, one individual—as the criterion by which the validity of political and social decisions is to be judged.

It is true, of course, that there would be no political or social institutions, nor any meaning to political enquiry, if men lived as single isolated individuals. To insist, as I do, that the individual is the criterion by which institutions and political theories should be judged is not to deny the immediate and obvious meaning of the phrase, "man is a social animal," that is, that each man has a multifarious set of relationships with other men.

The error arises when from this simple truism the conclusion is drawn that the set of relationships between men itself constitutes a real entity—an organism, as it were—called "society," with a life and with moral duties and rights of its own. This hypostatization of the sum of relations between men, this calling into being of an organism as the value center of political theory, is the essential note of the doctrines which underlie and inspire every powerful political movement of the twentieth century and all the effective transformations of political institutions which have taken place in the twentieth century.

By the nature of the case, if society is an organism, the men who make it up can be no more than cells in the body of society; and society, not they, becomes the criterion by which moral and political matters are judged. It is in society, not in the individuals who make it up, that right inheres; and whatever "rights" individual men may be allowed are pseudorights, granted and revocable by society. The moral claims of the person are in effect reduced to nothingness.

The Myth of Society

This, in one form or another, is the prevailing political doctrine of our time, a doctrine so widely and uncritically held that it has almost ceased to be doctrine and become a myth, largely below the level of conscious discourse. It is not thought about, but is itself constitutive of the forms of thought on political and social matters; and it establishes an atmosphere in which neither in political action nor in political thought are first principles considered—nor is the fundamental societarian premise itself critically assessed. This state of affairs is reflected almost universally—no less in the pronouncements of presidents, the judgments of the highest courts, and the deliberations of the Congress than in university lectures, learned journals, and scholarly studies.

It takes what is probably its most extreme form in the writings of the most influential schools of contemporary sociology.[4] Benjamin Schwartz, a sociologist himself, writing of certain trends among his colleagues, has epitomized what is in fact characteristic not only of most sociologists, but of most social scientists of all specialties. He attacks

> a natural tendency . . . to reduce the "isolated individual" to as rudimentary a model as possible, thus allowing full scope to social structure as a determining factor. Were it not for the annoying fact that the individual assumes the form of a biological organism, they might be able to claim him entirely.[5]

Or, as B. F. Skinner, professor of psychology at Harvard University, puts it:

> as the use of science increases, we are forced to accept the theoretical structure with which science represents its facts. . . . Every discovery of an event which has a part in shaping a man's behavior seems to leave so much the less to be credited to the man himself; and as such explanations become more and more comprehensive, the contributions which may be claimed by the individual himself appear to approach zero. Man's vaunted creative powers, his original accomplishments in art, science and morals, his capacity to

4. The indirect influence of this discipline upon political thought has been great for many decades. But if the example of the Supreme Court decision in the 1954 school segregation case, *Brown v. Board of Education*, is to be a precedent, that influence is now to become directly legislative; for in this case the Court in its decision relied primarily not upon principles of law, natural or positive, not upon Constitutional prescription or Congressional statute, but directly upon the theories of contemporary sociologists.

5. Benjamin Schwartz, "The Socio-Historic Approach," *World Politics* (October 1955): 134.

choose and our right to hold him responsible for the consequences of his choice—none of these is conspicuous in this new
self-portrait. Man, we once believed, was free to express himself in
art, music and literature, to inquire into nature, to seek salvation in
his own way. He could initiate action and make spontaneous and
capricious changes of course. Under the most extreme duress
some sort of choice remained to him. He could resist any effort to
control him, though it might cost him his life. But science insists
that action is initiated by forces impinging upon the individual,
and that caprice is only another name for behavior for which we
have not yet found a cause.[6]

science ultimately explains behavior in terms of "causes" or conditions which lie beyond the individual himself. As more and more
causal relations are demonstrated, a practical corollary becomes
difficult to resist: it should be possible to *produce* behavior according to plan simply by arranging the proper conditions.[7]

In turning to the external conditions which shape and maintain
the behavior of men, while questioning the reality of inner qualities and faculties to which human achievements were once [!] at-
tributed, we turn from the ill-defined and remote to the observable
and manipulable.[8]

The social engineering concept of the control of men for
purposes "scientifically" adumbrated and the collectivist concept which devalues men's status as individual persons for the
glorification of society and state are inherently interrelated.
And, curiously, considering the scientific and "value-free'
predilections of those who posit these associated concepts, a
third element always seems necessary to complete the symbi-
otic conceptual environment: "human welfare." This it is
which even so hard-boiled a proponent of "cultural engineer-

6. B. F. Skinner, "Freedom and the Control of Men," *American Scholar* (Winter 1955–56): 52–53.
7. Ibid., 47.
8. Ibid., 64–65.

ing" (his own term) as Professor Skinner presents as the end of his endeavors. But this, which one would think, being an end, should be the most firmly based of his concepts, is entirely vague—a mere pious decoration without content. The improvements in man towards which his engineering would be devoted relate to nothing in particular. What they are founded on "are not value judgments—they are guesses. To confuse and delay the improvement of cultural practices by quibbling about the word *improve* is itself not a useful practice."[9]

As with so many of his *compères,* academic and political, Professor Skinner's thought, skipping lightly over the undefined—and, it would appear, purely verbal—end of welfare, lands heavily upon the vital element of his conceptual apparatus: power. The words in which his dominant ideas are expressed are all derived from the rhetoric of power. His vision is one of "improving," "transforming," "controlling," "manipulating"—always by some unspecified elite (scientists, of course) operating upon other human beings.

Human beings considered as the objects of operations are no more nor less than . . . objects. Kant's imperative is reversed. Our humanitarians of the welfare society take this as their maxim: treat no person as an end, but only as a means to arrive at a general good.

Of course, it is not often that one finds so theoretically developed and uncompromising a statement as Professor Skinner's of the underlying beliefs upon which the liberal-collectivist *Weltanschauung* is based. This is for two reasons. In the first place, the positivist attitude and the admiration for the "value-free" methods of the natural sciences, which characterize the intellectual atmosphere, tend against the systematic statement of principle. The devaluation of the individual and the glorification of the collective are arrived at negatively: theoretically by a relativist criticism of the traditional value system and practically in the

9. Ibid., 50–51.

course of a variegated series of separate and detached social, economic, and political projects. The New Deal itself, which was decisive in the triumph of liberal collectivism in the United States, proceeded without any observable overall theory, by just such a series of projects. If one looks for general characteristics binding together these separate projects, one will find (apart from the fact that they all led towards an increase in the power of the state and a decrease in that of the person) only a sentimental mystique of welfare and a constant insistence upon the virtue of the pragmatic as over against the traditional ("horse-and-buggy economy for an automobile age").

In the second place, there still remains in the minds of the bearers of the contemporary relativist ideology a residue of absolute moral value, the heritage of their birth and upbringing in Western civilization, which is solidly based upon absolute value. The most relativist, the most instrumentalist of those who preach the mutability of morality would personally long hesitate before violating the moral principles he learned from the parents of his childhood or the church of his youth.[10] And similarly, when the blatant results of a naturalism free of the trammels of transcendent value are expressed socially in the logical rigor of totalitarian systems (which kill by wholesale for the sake of the Plan) or in juvenile delinquent gangs (which kill by retail for the sake of a thrill), they reject with horror phenomena which are entirely consistent with their philosophical position.[11] They are living on moral capital, their actions

10. So at least for the generation now dominant. What will be the case with *their* children, who have never had these experiences, is fearsome to contemplate.

11. I do not say the only type of phenomena consistent with it. Beneficent impulses leading spontaneously to beneficent acts would be just as consistent with it. The point is that neither bad impulses nor good ones, bad acts nor good ones, are inconsistent with a relativist philosophy, since there is no criterion of bad or good by which they can be judged—only an endless series of changes upon the theme of undirected efficacy: useful or nonuseful; instrumental or nonmeaningful—that is, not instrumental; socially directed or "destructive."

and attitudes modified by personal habits acquired under the tutelage of philosophies very different from theirs.

The Liberal-Collectivist Dogma

Nevertheless, however untheoretically stated, however inconsistently reflected in the actions of individuals in specific situations, a broadly consistent and delimitable body of dogma pervades the decisive and articulate sections of our society, shaping the minds of those who form opinion and create the conditions within which public decisions are made.

Philosophically, this body of dogma is relativist, pragmatic, positivist, scornful of absolute criteria, of all strictly theoretical thought, of all enquiry not amenable to the methods of the natural sciences.

Socially, it assumes the existence of an organism, "society," as the being to which, and to the good of which, all moral (and by the same token, political) problems finally refer. Sometimes this principle is modified, but never by intrinsic reference to the individual person, only (when the totalitarian implications of total reference to "society" loom too large) by reference to collectivist images of specialized groups of individuals: "minorities," "the underprivileged," "the elite," "scientists," "gifted children," "backward children," "labor." Concern is never for, there is no moral reference to, a man who is a Negro, a poor man, a rich man, a well-born man, an able man, a biologist, a child, a carpenter.

Politically, it attributes virtue in strict proportionality to power. Actions are best, and best performed, when the state performs them; and within the governmental structure, best when the act of the federal government rather than of the several states; and within the federal government, best when the action of the executive rather than of the legislature. And if it cannot be the act of government, better that it be the act of an organization than that of an individual, better that of a large organization than that of a small one. Virtue resides infinitely more in the United Steel Workers of America than in any individual steelworker; more in the NAACP than in any individual colored person; more in the AAUP than in any university professor, however distinguished.

Economically, it takes for granted that the several energies of men expressed through the functioning of a free-market economy can lead only to disaster (although it was with the growth of that system that the great leap in human productivity of the last 150 years occurred). Considering centralized direction and regulation the desideratum of economic systems, it either looks towards state ownership of all productive facilities, in a Marxist or quasi-Marxist manner, or, in a Keynesian manner, it demands that in a "mixed economy" the state control all the decisive sectors of the economy and receive a lion's share, through taxation, of the product. In either case it insists that only "socially desirable" production shall be encouraged and that the decision as to what is "socially desirable" shall be made not by individual consumers through the market, but by bureaucrats and social workers through the power of regulation and taxation.

Emotionally, it prefers psychoanalysis to the dark night of the soul, "adjustment" to achievement, security to freedom. It preaches "the end of ideology," admires experts and fears prophets, fears above all commitment to value transcending the fact.

These, broadly stated, are the tenets of the prevailing liberal-collectivist orthodoxy.

The New Conservatism

It is in challenge to this orthodoxy that the movement of thought which has come to be called the New Conservatism presents itself. The New Conservatism is a palpable body of opinion, but a body of opinion which it is somewhat difficult to delimit. It has no organization; it has issued no manifesto; some of its leading spokesmen, indeed, never use the phrase "New Conservatism," but prefer to speak of "a conservatism of reflection" or "enlightened conservatism." It is nonetheless a coherent and reasonably specific set of political theories projected by an intellectually influential group. It is recognized as a definite school of thought not only by other political theorists and in academic and critical circles generally, but also in the wider world.

Peter Viereck, Clinton Rossiter, and Russell Kirk are its most widely recognized interpreters; and, of these, Kirk is undoubtedly the most influential. It is to him that I shall most frequently refer in my discussion of the New Conservatism, as the most typical and authoritative champion of its position and its mode of thought.[12]

These are the best known of those who have worked out the New Conservative position; but there are a considerable number of other scholars whose contributions to this body of thought are of great importance, and I shall have occasion from time to time to refer to them. A list, by no means exhaustive, of the more distinguished of these might include such names as Robert A. Nisbet, John H. Hallowell, the late Gordon K. Chalmers, Thomas I. Cook, and Peter Drucker. One might go on indefinitely, particularly if account were taken of those who exist in the vague penumbra of the New Conservative influence. Publicists like Walter Lippmann reflect some of its ideas. Even active participants in the liberal-collectivist political world, like George Kennan, Reinhold Niebuhr, and August Heckscher, frequently

---

12. I refer to Mr. Kirk's fundamental position, as developed in his major works, *The Conservative Mind* (Chicago: Henry Regnery, 1953) and *A Program for Conservatives* (Chicago: Henry Regnery, 1954), and also in his writings up to very recently. In the last year or two, however, in a number of his contributions to periodicals, there has been observable some weakening in his intransigent New Conservative position and some sign of a greater sympathy with the position of the American conservative consensus on individual freedom.

use a rhetoric, and sometimes concepts, not unlike those of the
New Conservatism.

Just as it shades off on the one hand into the platitudes of
editorialists for "modern Republicanism" or the rhetoric of
sated New Dealers in a mood to consolidate the Roosevelt revolution and sanctify it with a conservative aura, so on the other
hand it sometimes is confused with the very different approaches of such conservative analysts of political philosophy
as Eric Voegelin, Leo Strauss, and Willmoore Kendall, or of
such critics as Richard Weaver and Frederick Wilhelmsen.[13]
But these latter scholars are distinguished from the New Conservatives by the much greater intransigence of their criticism
of collectivist liberalism and by a radically different philosophical attitude. The high value they place upon the faculty of reason for the establishing of conservative principles separates
them sharply from the New Conservatives, who insist upon the
undifferentiated virtue of tradition, not merely as guide and
governor of reason, but over against reason.

The Place of Principle

This attitude towards reason is the characteristic methodological sign of the New Conservatism, which elevates the historical
process, the venerable, the established, the prescriptive, as the
touchstone of the good and the true. While the process of history is seen as Providential dispensation and the intellectual
appeal is to the tradition of Burke, the mode of thought is that

13. Likewise, I do not consider among the New Conservatives those English
or Continental writers who are sometimes grouped with them: such men as
Michael Oakeshott, the late Lord Percy of Newcastle, Bertrand de Jouvenel,
Erik von Kuehnelt-Leddihn, as well as Wilhelm Roepke and his "neoliberal"
associates. The European situation differs so sharply from the American that
even those like Michael Oakeshott, who are closest to the attitudes of the New
Conservatism, represent a rather different phenomenon; and most of these
men are even further removed from its position.

which was brought to its highest perfection by Hegel; and as a mode of thought, it suffers from the same innate difficulties as does the Hegelian.

These men are not statesmen like Burke; the prudential choice between immediate practical alternatives, which is the proper task of the statesman, leads in the scholar, the political theorist, to a theoretical impasse. It is one thing for the impassioned author of *Reflections on the Revolution in France,* the defender of a powerful, a solid constitution, not seriously challenged at home, to depend upon the traditional existence of that constitution as its sole sanction and warrant. But the New Conservatives are concerned with the salvation of their civilization and their country from positivist and liberal-collectivist doctrines which are already far advanced in authority over the minds and hearts of men. The values they purport to defend *are* seriously challenged at home. To make *their* sole sanction prescription, to condemn the effort to judge society by theoretical standards, to disparage the exercise of the faculty of reason in that effort as "abstract speculation" and "defecated rationality"—this is to put themselves at the mercy of the very forces they are proposing to combat. It leaves them in a dilemma from which there is no logical escape.

Either the whole historical and social situation in which they find themselves, including the development of collectivism, statism, and intellectual anarchy, is Providential, and all prescriptive attitudes, including the orthodox collectivist attitudes of the day, are right and true: in which case there is no justification for their stand as an opposition. Or, there is a higher sanction than prescription and tradition; there are standards of truth and good by which men must make their ultimate judgment of ideas and institutions; in which case, reason, operating against the background of tradition, is the faculty upon which they must depend in making that judgment.

It is the same dilemma as that created by the Hegelian dictum "all that is real is rational." Nor is Hegel's own mystical escape from the impasse available to the New Conservatives, who do not accept his dialectic. Within the limits of the complex and powerful myth which he created, he could confute the obvious—that much that exists is irrational—by denying the reality of phenomena which contradicted his thesis, by pairing with "all that is real is rational" the parallel statement, "all that is rational is real."

Such refinements do not exist in the Burkean heritage. Although the particular form that Burke's thinking took at the historical moment in which he found himself is undoubtedly in the direct ancestry of Hegel's system,[14] Burke himself was too much the hard-headed Englishman to have sought such a solution, had he faced the sort of problem his *soi-disant* heirs do. He would have been more likely, I believe, in conditions such as ours today to have drawn upon the other, the submerged side of his thinking, his fundamental belief in natural rights and in reason as their interpreter. And this, I think, he also would have done, had he lived in 1688, at the time of the revolution whose established results he celebrates prescriptively a hundred years later. In his struggle against the French Revolution and its perversion of the doctrine of natural rights, this aspect of his thinking fell into desuetude, but it was always there in the background, giving foundation and firmness to his exercise of prudence and expedience.

Our contemporary Burkeans will, of course, have none of the Hegelian mysticism; and they continue to reject the appeal to principle, even in the terms that Burke might have allowed. The only way out of their impasse is the way they take: to deny

14. "Prescription cannot be the sole authority for a constitution, and therefore recourse to rights anterior to the constitution, i.e., to natural rights, cannot be superfluous unless prescription by itself is a sufficient guaranty of goodness. Transcendent standards can be dispensed with if the standard is inherent in the process; 'the actual and the present is the rational.' What could appear as a return to the primeval equation of the good with the ancestral is, in fact, a preparation for Hegel." Leo Strauss, *Natural Right and History* (Chicago: University of Chicago Press, 1953), 319.

that it is an impasse, to insist that the great tradition of the West is still dominant in the West. Despite the evidence of their senses, they brush away the prevailing power of the outlook which is in fact dominant in the schools and universities, dominant in the mass-communications industries, dominant in the bureaucracy of government, dominant in every decisive position in the land.

By denying the immense and tragic impact of the revolution in accepted ways of thought that the past half century—and particularly the years since 1932—has brought forth, they are saved the need for recourse to principle. The wave of the present which seems to be carrying us towards the questionable alternative of a *Brave New World* or a *1984,* they can pooh-pooh as nothing but evanescent ripples, froth created by a few already discredited "defecated intellectuals." All that is necessary to return to health and sanity, they insist, is to ignore these temporary and feeble ripples of opinion.

Every twist of the radio or television dial, every turn of the pages of the daily paper or of our magazines, highbrow, lowbrow, or middlebrow, every act of our governors reflects those opinions. This is a new "tradition," which, if unchallenged, will eclipse the long tradition of America and the West, less crudely than Orwell's Ministry of Truth destroyed history in the interests of a ruling oligarchy, but as effectively. Between the claims of a newly imposed prescriptive outlook, heir to two hundred years or more of "enlightened" naysaying to the possibility of truth, and the claims of the older tradition upon which this Republic was founded, the tradition of Greece and Israel and Christianity, only a choice based upon principle can decide. But to the patent facts of contemporary history, they turn their blind eye.

To recognize that there is a need to distinguish between traditions, to choose between the good and the evil in tradition, requires recognition of the preeminent role (not, lest I be misunderstood, the sole role) of reason in distinguishing among the possibilities which have been open to men since the serpent tempted Eve and Adam ate of the Tree of the Knowledge of Good and Evil. But this is exactly what the New Conservatives refuse to recognize. The refusal to recognize the role of reason, the refusal to acknowledge that, in the immense flow of tradition, there are in fact diverse elements that must be distinguished on a principled basis and considered in their relationship to present realities, is a central attribute of New Conservative thought.

It is this which separates the New Conservatism from the conservatism of principle that rejects Burke and the Burkean approach, since being "grounded in the nature of a situation rather than in the nature of things, its opposition will not be a dialectically opposed opposition."[15] The proponents of the conservatism of principle see that the coherent and comprehensive character of the ascendant thought of the day is not to be countered by anything less than an opposition of principle, which digs to the theoretical roots, indulging necessarily in what Burke called "metaphysical distinctions"—adding, "I hate the very sound of them."[16]

Burke, like his followers, raised the virtue of prudence, the faculty that adapts general principles to concrete circumstances, to an independent and decisive place. There, instead of complementing the role of reason in political thought, it reduces political thought to what our contemporary sociologists would call "situational analysis." It is for this reason that Richard Weaver says:

> Burke should not be taken as prophet by the political conservatives. True, he has left many wonderful materials which they should assimilate. His insights into human nature are quite solid propositions to build with, and his eloquence is a lesson for all time in the

15. Richard M. Weaver, *The Ethics of Rhetoric* (Chicago: Henry Regnery, 1953), 83.
16. *The Works of Edmund Burke*, Bohn ed., vol. 1 (London: George Bell & Sons, 1902), 432.

effective power of energy and imagery. Yet these are the auxiliary rhetorical appeals. For the rhetorical appeal on which it will stake its life, a cause must have some primary source of argument which will not be embarrassed by abstractions or even by absolutes—the general ideas mentioned by Tocqueville. Burke was magnificent at embellishment, but of clear rational principle he had a mortal distrust. It could almost be said that he raised "muddling through" to the height of a science, though in actuality it can never be a science. In the most critical undertaking of all, the choice of one's source of argument, it would be blindness to take him as mentor.[17]

The dread of definition, of distinction, of clear rational principle is characteristic of the New Conservatism. Telling though many of its criticisms are—of the aridity, the "other-directedness," the materialism of the contemporary scene—the New Conservatism is self-disarmed in its chosen task. Rejection of the weapon of reason forecloses the possibility of a consistent and cogent attack upon the liberal-collectivist philosophy which lies behind those conditions.

The concept of Providence, upon which New Conservative political thought depends, is undoubtedly an essential part of the Western and Christian tradition. But in this tradition the concept of God's Providence as immanent, as operating within the flow of historical experience, is always in tension with the concept of God as transcendent, as the ground and standard of truth and good. When, however, the concept of Providence appears as a determining factor in the political theory of the New Conservatism—most explicitly in the writings of Russell Kirk, but implicitly in all the arguments of the New Conservatives—it is overwhelmingly immanentist. That is to say, it assumes that the Divine Will is expressed *in* the march of events, and therefore that it is *to* the march of events, to history and the tradition embodied in history, that we must look for the ground and standard of truth and good.

17. Weaver, *The Ethics of Rhetoric*, 83–84.

Ultimately, no doubt, there is a difference between this concept of history as the expression of the immanent working of Providence and the positivist identification of what ought to be with what is, of truth with experience. But methodologically, in the field of political theory, they are similar. Both reject the necessity of a disciplined philosophical establishment of criteria by which political societies should be judged. Both deny that such an enquiry is necessarily prior to all prudential judging of actuality. Both, that is, elevate the practical act of judgment—which should be based on theory and principle—to the be-all and end-all of political thought.

It is true that abstract theoretical principles cannot be applied without consideration of circumstances, of the possibilities which in fact exist at a given time. That, however, does not mean that prudence can successfully function without the guidance of reason. It does not mean that because concrete circumstances *affect* the application of principle, they therefore *replace* principle and become the sole determinant of political theory. Action based upon political theory thus empirically conceived becomes the sheerest expediency, with no end or purpose but to maneuver upon the wave of the present. The rejection of reason and principle as decisive factors leaves no other course open.

The Necessity of Freedom

As a result, New Conservative thought can give no more substantial meaning to freedom than can the positivism against which it arrays itself. There is a dichotomy between historical experience as a theater in which men work out their drama and the transcendent standard of truth and good from which that drama takes meaning. If this dichotomy is not recognized, then there can be no choice, and with no choice, no freedom. Either men must go willingly in the direction in which history moves, or they will go unwillingly. *Ducunt Fata volentem, nolentem trahunt.* Only if there exists a real choice between right and wrong, truth and error, a choice which can be made irrespective of the direction in which history and impersonal Fate move, do men possess true freedom.

This is the meaning of the lines from the inscription above the Gate of Hell in Dante's *Inferno*, lines which ever remain a stumbling block to anyone, atheist or theist, who will not see that the glory of man's being is that he is free to choose good or evil, truth or error:

> Giustizia mosse il mio alto Fattore;
>   fecemi la divina Potestate,
>   la somma Sapienza *e il primo Amore*

> Justice moved my great Maker; the Power of God,
>   His supreme Wisdom and *His primal Love* created me.

The words I have emphasized are the boggling point: primal Love. And they are made more scandalous still if one attempts to illuminate them in the light of a sentence from a contemporary Christian apologist (I have forgotten from whom, but it was probably Charles Williams or C. S. Lewis): "Hell is God's last gift to man." But freedom can exist at no lesser price than the danger of damnation; and if freedom is indeed the essence of man's being, that which distinguishes him from the beasts, he must be free to choose his worst as well as his best end. Unless he can choose his worst, he cannot *choose* his best.

No philosophical position that looks to the flow of existence as the sole standard of judgment has any place for true choice. It does not, for this purpose, matter whether the flow of existence is regarded as expressing Divine Providence or the dialectical play of the Absolute, or is thought of as self-contained, nonteleological, a simple positivist assemblage of data. The decisive point is that for any of these positions, freedom can only mean some variation on the Hegelian "freedom is the recognition of necessity." The content of necessity may be variously conceived; it may be regarded as the immutable objective development of the ideal (Hegel), or as an immanent Providence (Kirk), or simply as that which is (the positivists). But, however "necessity" is regarded, to define freedom as recognition, understanding, acceptance of it, is to make the concept of freedom meaningless. Such "recognition" is not a moral act, an act of choice, an act of the will; it has nothing to do with choice. All that is involved is sufficient understanding to know in what direction things are moving, which way one will be dragged if one does not willingly go along. For the human person this is not freedom; it is external determination of his life. It is a heads-I-win, tails-you-lose proposition. It reduces him from a person whose understanding enlightens his will by bringing existence before the bar of essential principle to a somewhat exalted IBM machine, which registers what experiential existence feeds into it and makes prudential judgments accordingly.

The person, the free human being, is one who can maneuver on the wave of the present if he finds it good, but who will set his face resolutely against it if he finds it bad—even though in a material and practical sense this latter course means that he will be dashed to pieces on the rocks. There are times when the choice which is the expression of freedom as it affects immediate action may be reduced to just so simple an alternative. But even then, morally and spiritually (and in the long run of history, often practically) that choice is a real choice.

The calculating machine can only decide unerringly for security, for survival, for acquiescence in what is and what is becoming. The human being can say quite simply—and literally: To Hell with it; it is wrong and it is false, and in my inner being I will have no part of it, whatever may be forced upon me physically. Fitzjames Stephen, his deeper insights, as they sometimes did, breaking through the utilitarian structure of his thought, has put the matter with all succinctness: "The waters are out and no human force can turn them back, but I do not see why as we go with the stream we need sing Hallelujah to the river god."[18] Sometimes the choice available may be no more than this, to refuse to acquiesce. But such a choice is impossible when reason and principle are scorned, when virtue is reduced to prudence, when the search for truth is castigated as abstract speculation.

In less extreme situations also, freedom in its true sense, the exercise of choice, is ruled out by the position the New Conservatives maintain. To be sure, they talk a good deal about freedom, as do also the liberal-collectivist positivists and the Hegelians; but when they speak of freedom they mean doing what has to be done or what ought to be done. Freedom never means to them the only thing it can mean if it is not to be reduced to necessity or duty. But necessity and duty are perfectly adequate concepts and there is no reason why they cannot carry the weight of their own meaning. Freedom means freedom: not necessity, but choice; not responsibility, but the choice between responsibility and irresponsibility; not duty, but the choice between accepting and rejecting duty; not virtue, but the choice between virtue and vice.

Freedom and Its Uses

I am not defending blind and frivolous action, irresponsibility, immorality, or amorality. I believe there are absolute truths and absolute values towards which men should direct themselves. I am only insisting that freedom cannot be defined in terms of the ends that a free person ought to choose, that freedom, which is the power to choose, cannot be identified with what is chosen.

This may seem so self-evident as hardly to need argument; but, unfortunately, it always has and it continues to. As for

18. James Fitzjames Stephen, *Liberty, Equality, Fraternity* (London: Smith, Elder, and Co., 1873), 242.

Hegel "freedom is the recognition of necessity," and for the rationalist "freedom is freedom to do the right," and for the scientificist freedom is an illusion cloaking the materially determined character of all human responses, so in a parallel manner the New Conservative continuously and strenuously reduces freedom to meaninglessness.

John Hallowell, for example, writes:

> A new social philosophy . . . will recognize that freedom is directed toward ends more ultimate than freedom itself. For freedom is not an end in itself . . . but an essential means to the development of moral and spiritual perfection. *And it loses its meaning and degenerates into license if it is not directed toward that end.*[19] [My emphasis, F.S.M.]

His argument is typical of the attitude of the New Conservatism towards the concept of freedom. To the implied questions, what is freedom? and is it valuable?, he replies with an elaborate begging of the questions. What he says amounts to this: (1) Freedom which is not utilized to achieve right ends "is an empty kind of freedom." (2) Since it is only a means to a given set of ends, if it is used for any other purpose than the achievement of those ends, it becomes something else, something which is neither defined nor characterized except by being given an ugly name, "license."

The difficulty is that the rose by the ugly name smells just as sweet. Freedom-license remains the unrestrained power to choose—whether the choice made is good or bad. Of the nature of freedom the argument tells us nothing, for it splits the very concept it is presumably defining and judging, defining it differently and judging it differently not in accordance with any difference of essence, but solely in accordance with the accidental and external question of how it is used. A rose is not a stinkweed because it gives some people rose fever. In thus refusing to consider freedom as a unitary concept, Mr. Hallo-

---

19. John H. Hallowell, *The Moral Foundation of Democracy* (Chicago: University of Chicago Press, 1954), 87.

well avoids the difficult problem of the relation of freedom to the end of moral and spiritual perfection.

For moral and spiritual perfection can only be pursued by finite men through a series of choices, in which every moment is a new beginning; and the freedom which makes those choices possible is itself a condition without which the moral and spiritual ends would be meaningless. If this were not so, if such ends could be achieved without the continuing exercise of freedom, then moral and spiritual perfection could be taught by rote and enforced by discipline—and every man of good will would be a saint. Freedom is therefore an integral aspect of the highest end. It is also, to be sure, an integral aspect of the lowest end, of total rejection of good and truth. If this is paradoxical, it is the paradox of the human condition. But paradox or no paradox, it remains true that freedom is not subordinate to moral and spiritual ends; rather it is concomitant with them, for without freedom no moral end can be achieved by the particular kind of being man is. Freedom that is not used to achieve high ends does not become something else; it does not change into another entity, "license." It is simply freedom that is not used to achieve high ends, freedom badly used; but it is still freedom. A hammer when you smash your thumb with it is just as much a hammer as when you drive a nail true.

The refusal to distinguish freedom from the ends towards which the free human being ought to move, the insistence that freedom badly used is not freedom but an indefinite something called license, is repeated again and again in the literature of the New Conservatism. Russell Kirk, in an essay called "Conditions of Freedom,"[20] skips hither and yon through the pages of intellectual history, bringing authority to bear from Greece and India, from Israel and Christendom; it is a perfectly good argument for what men ought to do, but it says nothing about freedom. It only attempts by its rhetoric to con-

---

20. Russell Kirk, *Beyond the Dreams of Avarice* (Chicago: Henry Regnery, 1956), 166–72.

vey to the reader that freedom is doing what one ought to do. Nowhere is there an attempt to consider freedom as choice and to come to grips with the problems of the "conditions of freedom" that arise if freedom is so understood. Freedom in this sense, the only sense in which it retains meaning, is dismissed with a quotation from Milton at his most polemical and most personally aggrieved, a quotation from an outburst entitled "On the Detraction which followed upon my writing certain Treatises":

> This is got by casting pearls to hogs,
> That bawl for *freedom* in their senseless mood,
> And still revolt when truth would set them free.
> License they mean when they cry *liberty;*
> For who loves that, must first be wise and good.

The same Milton, however, when he wrote soberly and seriously on this question in the *Areopagitica*, magnificently vindicated the thesis that freedom to choose is the very essence of the pursuit of virtue:

It was from out the rind of one apple tasted, that the knowledge of good and evil as two twins cleaving together leaped forth into the World. And perhaps this is that doom which Adam fell into of knowing good and evil, that is to say of knowing good by evil. As therefore the state of man now is; what wisdom can there be to choose, what continence to forbear without the knowledge of evil? He that can apprehend and consider vice with all her baits and seeming pleasures, and yet abstain, and yet distinguish, and yet prefer that which is truly better, he is the true wayfaring Christian. I cannot praise a fugitive and cloistered virtue, unexercised and unbreathed, that never sallies out and sees her adversary, but slinks out of the race, where that immortal garland is to be run for, not without dust and heat. Assuredly we bring not innocence into the world, we bring impurity much rather: that which purifies us is trial, and trial is by what is contrary.[21]

21. *Milton's Prose,* The World's Classics, ed. Malcolm W. Wallace, no. 293 (London: Oxford University Press, 1925), 290.

This is the Milton of the great epic poems of freedom and its uses, good and evil, not the peevish polemicist of sectarian struggle. It is the Milton who celebrates freedom, understanding that for an innocent being, or for a perfect one, virtue is so natural that choice is without meaning, but that for a human being it is choice and its freedom that is the prime condition of virtue: "As therefore the state of man now is; what wisdom can there be to choose, what continence to forbear without knowledge of evil? . . . that which purifies us [that is, brings us to virtue] is trial, and trial is by what is contrary."

But Mr. Kirk's entire essay bears with all its weight in the opposite direction. Freedom is again and again confused with virtuous ends: "submission to the will of God"; "the absence of desire"; reconciliation "with the demands of social cooperation." Implicitly and explicitly, under the guise of a discussion of freedom, it is a plea for virtue, neglecting utterly the essence of freedom.

The Recalcitrance of Freedom

It is simple enough to come forth with a solution of the dilemma of freedom and virtue if freedom of choice as the condition of achieving virtue is ignored and if freedom is reduced to acceptance of that which is right.

The trouble is that freedom is more recalcitrant. It is the condition of virtue, but it is also the condition of vice. It is not true, as Russell Kirk says, that "the true freedom of the person . . . subsists in community";[22] it subsists in the individual. He may find freedom in communal participation, or he may find it in ignoring community, even in revolt against community. It all depends upon the circumstances; but what does not depend upon the circumstances is the necessity of freedom. Freedom can and may be in accord with social order; it can and may be

22. Kirk, "Ethical Labor," in *Beyond the Dreams of Avarice,* 99.

in disaccord. There is no preestablished harmony; it all hangs upon the character of the social order.

The problem of political theory and political practice is to bring about such conditions of order as make possible the greatest exercise of freedom by the individual. But that problem cannot be solved so long as the potential opposition between freedom and virtue is passed over and freedom is defined in terms that ignore its essence and verbally remove the possibility of opposition.

In the "progressive" cant of the past few decades, the confusion inherent in this view of freedom has been expressed in the phrase "not freedom *from*, but freedom *for*." The "freedom from" here deprecated is freedom in its true meaning. The "freedom for" is not freedom at all, but simply a set of ends conceived as the proper purpose of freedom. While the ends posited in this argument differ profoundly from those propounded by the New Conservatives ("freedom for" being usually conceived in terms of jobs, security, and the rest of the materialist Bill of Claims), this attitude reflects the same conceptual rejection of integral freedom. Neither the welfare-statist with his materialist ends nor the New Conservative with his spiritual ends is willing to accept freedom. The word, however, is a good word, a "God-term" in Richard Weaver's terminology; and both make play with it. But neither is willing to face the conclusion that acceptance of freedom in its true meaning would force upon him: that freedom does not lead inexorably and of itself to the ends which either of them espouses, but only makes it possible for each individual person to choose between them.

In pressing the credentials of freedom, I am not maintaining that these two sets of ends are equally valid. Far from it. I regard the moral and spiritual virtues as—by all rational, prescriptive, and intuitive evidence—demonstrably the true end of man. I regard the materialist positivist Utopia to be *as an end* a lure to man's degradation (however useful material well-being is when held in due proportion). But the issue in the analysis of freedom is not the validity of the respective ends of the two parties, but their common denial that man can reach a worthy end only if he is free to reject it, that "that which purifies us is trial, and trial is by what is contrary."

Clinton Rossiter in his *Conservatism in America,* discussing the problems of liberty and security in modern society, hopes that "the new conservatism" may give us a "firmer grasp of the relationship" between them; riding over the problems that exist if liberty—freedom—is seriously considered, he says:

> Orators of the Right will continue to make capital out of the false polarity between these two most powerful of man's desires. . . .[23]

In the manner I have been analyzing, he proceeds to reduce the meaning of liberty to that which achieves the ends he posits under the shibboleth-word "security." He at least does it quite openly:

> The conservative should give us a definition of liberty that is positive and all-embracing, not negative and narrow. In the new conservative dictionary, *liberty* will be defined with the help of words like *opportunity, creativity, productivity,* and *security.*[24]

Whatever one may think of these ends (and despite their noble sound, some of them as generalizations conceal rather extensive minefields); even if it could be admitted that as ends they are unexceptionable and representative of the highest good—they still in no way help to define liberty or freedom. Freedom could be as well, or as badly, defined by substituting *rugged individualism* or *hierarchy* for *opportunity, love* or *duty* for *creativity, asceticism* for *productivity, adventure* for *security.* One could indeed continue to ring an indefinite number of changes on this note—as many as the ends which men have

---

23. Clinton Rossiter, *Conservatism in America* (New York: Alfred A. Knopf, 1955), 257.
24. Ibid., 258. Italics in original.

chosen and the interpretations they have given to these ends. But no group of them, nor all of them taken together, can help to define freedom or liberty, certainly not to "give us a definition . . . that is positive and all-embracing, not negative and narrow." For freedom is *not* "all-embracing." It is a specific aspect of the condition of man; it is neutral to ends—and presumably, therefore, "narrow"; and it is as "negative" as it is "positive," since its exercise demands that it reject all alternatives but the one it chooses.

One can sympathize with the effort on the part of political theorists to reduce the meaning of freedom and equate it with the ends the reductionist accepts as virtue. To do so eliminates a stubborn problem: the resolution of the dilemma of freedom and virtue, the resolution of the contradiction between man's nature as a radically free being and the exigencies of that necessary political order without which neither freedom nor virtue could long flourish. But the dilemma thus resolved is illegitimately resolved. It can be resolved, as I hope to demonstrate, but not by eliminating freedom, for freedom is essential to the being of man.

4

WHAT KIND OF ORDER?

O rder" is the battle cry of those who deny that freedom is the aspect of the nature of men which political institutions exist to serve. "Order," they insist, not freedom, is the primary reason for the existence of those institutions, the first criterion by which they should be judged. Now, of course, there can be no denial that men can live as men only in some relationship with other men and that the sum of all the relations between men will make up some form of order. The form may vary from a quasi anarchy to the most iron of authoritarian regimes, but some form it will have. So far, those who preach the importance of the concept of "order" in political theory are right; but so far what they stress is no more than a truism.

The key word is "some." Some order there will be always. What is important is not order as order but what kind of order. The task of political theory is to develop the criteria by which differing political orders can be judged in the light of principle. The mere fact that to exist man must live under *some* political order cannot be itself the standard by which the character of an order may be judged. The problem rather is *what* political order, in the circumstances of any given place and era, will best conduce to the establishment and preservation of conditions most favorable to the pursuit of the ends of man's existence.

The New Conservative differs from the collectivist liberal as to the nature of these ends. He rejects the contemporary orthodoxy which is based upon the idea that man is but a tool-bearing gregarious animal whose end is material welfare; in the tradition of the West, he posits as the end of man the pursuit of virtue. Where he fails to differentiate himself, however, from those he opposes is in his acceptance of the idea that ends are implicit in the flux of experience. Whether that flux be thought of as materialist or Providential, and whether therefore the ends it dictates are material or ideal, both notions lead to the denial of the possibility of choice and freedom. And from this denial arises the concept of a political order where power rests of right in the hands of those who understand the true ends of existence, of those who can force men to be, in the one case, materially happy, in the other case, virtuous.

Freedom is reduced to understanding what the Fates decree. While all men understand, some men understand more than others; and those who understand the most must force those who understand less to understand more. We are back with Rousseau: "men must be forced to be free." But, as I have tried to demonstrate, men are made in such a way that they can make no ends their own except through free choice. Men cannot be forced to be free, nor can they even be forced to be virtuous. To a certain extent, it is true, they can be forced to act as though they were virtuous. But virtue is the fruit of well-used freedom. And no act to the degree that it is coerced can partake of virtue—or of vice.

Thus there remains a problem, and a very real one for the political theorist. If virtue is the true end of man's existence, if it can only be achieved in freedom, and if freedom by its nature can lead to vice as well as to virtue, what, then, of the criterion of the political order? There is undoubtedly a dilemma posed. The contradiction in the condition of man—that he can only achieve the good if he is free to reject it—has its reflection in the political sphere. The political enforcement of the good is only possible if the freedom which men must have to seek the good is destroyed.

Approaches to the Dilemma of Freedom and Virtue

In discussing this problem, the general approach of political theory, since its beginnings in Plato, has not been essentially different from the one I have been analyzing, the approach which the New Conservatives share with the collectivist liberals. Freedom has been subordinated to the ends designated as good by the theorist, and the criterion of the good society and the good political order has been their consonance with those ends.

Doubts have arisen about this cavalier treatment of freedom, but in the main line of political thought little attention has been paid to them until, within the last two hundred years, a school of thought arose that reversed the evasion of the contradiction to substitute another evasion, placing the freedom of the individual not simply as the criterion of political order, but as the sole good and end of existence. Radically secularist in its philosophical assumptions and positivist in its negation of absolute value, it turned "freedom is freedom to do the right" into "make men free and they will do the right," the right being implicitly defined as what free men will do. This solution of the problem, which is approximately that which Bentham and the two Mills held in common with so many of the political thinkers of the century they epitomized, also evades rather than faces the contradiction. The ends of human existence can no more, with respect for reality, be subordinated to freedom than freedom to those ends.

Resolution of the Dilemma

Is there, then, no solution? Must we either accept the reality of freedom and deny objective value or accept objective value and deny the reality of freedom? I would maintain not only that there is a solution but also that it has been approximated in practice in a number of political societies and most closely by the United States in the original conception of its Founding Fathers. I would also maintain that theoretically that solution has been touched on again and again,[25] although rarely, except in the American Constitutional debates, has it been developed as the central concept of a political theory.

The dilemma is one which can only be solved by the classical logical device of grasping it by both horns. For the difficulty is that both its major premises are true: on the one hand, freedom *is* essential to the nature of man and neutral to virtue and vice; on the other hand, good ends *are* good ends, and it *is* the duty of man to pursue them. I deny only that in the real situation with which we are dealing these two true premises are contradictories. Rather they are axioms true of different though interconnected realms of existence. How can true ends be established elsewhere than in the intellectual, the moral, the spiritual order? Where can the conditions for freedom be established but in the social order, which means—since this is where determining force centers—in the political order? A good society is possible only when both these conditions are met: when the social and political order guarantees a state of affairs in which men can freely choose and when the intellectual and moral leaders, the "creative minority," have the understanding and imagination to maintain the prestige of tradition and reason, and thus to sustain the intellectual and moral order throughout society.

To the degree that either of these conditions is lacking, a society will not be a good society, and the individual men who constitute it will suffer in their humanity. Granted the highest development of freedom in the political order, a failure of the responsible interpreters of the intellectual, moral, and spiritual order would make freedom a useless toy by depriving men of

25. In America, for example, by Madison and Calhoun, in England by Acton and Percy, to mention only one or two. Even in the Greek world, Aristotle occasionally approaches the solution, although his basic position is far from it.

standards by which to guide their lives. On the other hand, given the most elevated intellectual, moral, and spiritual understanding, the subordination of the political order to the enforcement of that understanding, the denial to men of the freedom to accept it or reject it, would make virtue meaningless and truth rote.

There exist, therefore, two problems; but only one of them, the problem of the conditions of a good political order, is the concern of political theory in the strict sense and therefore the direct subject of this book. There are of course interpenetrations between the spheres, effects upon each sphere from developments in the other. The very concept of freedom as the essential condition of the development of human beings depends upon propositions drawn from the intellectual and spiritual order. Deformations in the political order make the preservation, growth, and propagation of fundamental truth extremely difficult. But they still remain separate realms, and the criteria of the two orders are very different.

Political theory and practice, therefore, must be judged by criteria proper to the political order; and the decisive criterion of any political order is the degree to which it establishes conditions of freedom. On the political and social level this is primary. Much could be said about the causes and remedies of the intellectual and spiritual *malaise* of our time, but that is the subject matter of another book; here I shall be able only to touch upon it briefly in a later chapter.

Rights and Duties

Once this necessary separation of spheres is understood, it becomes clear what is wrong with the cardinal objection the New Conservatives bring against a politics of freedom: the argument that the rights of individuals are not unalienable, that they must be subordinated to the performance of duties. If the relation of rights and duties as a political problem is considered under the criteria of the political sphere, the falsity of this doctrine becomes apparent. The individual person lives in a social milieu constituted of other persons and groupings of persons who make up social and political institutions. However much awe and reverence may rightly or wrongly become associated with these institutions, they cannot *as such* have any moral claims upon him. Only insofar as they represent the moral claims of other persons, that is, only secondarily, does he have duties to them. The Great Commandment, which is the cornerstone of the structure of Western moral thought, reflects this hierarchy of values, ignoring utterly everything but God and individual persons: "Thou shalt love the Lord thy God with all thy heart, and with all thy soul, and with all thy strength, and with all thy mind; and thy neighbour as thyself."

If particular social institutions, which are composed of more or less determinable groups of persons, are secondary and their claims derivative, then even less can "society," which is simply an abstraction of the sum total of all the relations between persons, be a primary source of obligation in moral and political thought. When the New Conservative insists with Burke on the claims of "this mysterious incorporation of the human race," one of two things follows. Either he must actually believe that society is a living organism, endowed with a soul and constituting a third term that should be added to the Great Commandment, or he is talking nonsense.

Only if he is willing to take the former position is it possible logically to defend as an axiom of political theory the proposition, no rights without corresponding duties. This doctrine, much older of course than the New Conservatism, has taken many forms; but in all its forms, as in New Conservative thought, it depends upon the belief that society or the state is a being, almost a person, who in reciprocal relationship with individual persons hands out rights as they fulfill their duties to it. In such a scheme of things, "rights" would obviously be dependent upon duties performed; but they would not be rights, they would be privileges. The rights of human beings, however, are not the gift of some Leviathan; they are inherently derived from the nature of men. The duties of human beings are not tribute owed to Leviathan; they are moral imperatives grounded in objective value. Each is independent of the other; it is not a matter of *quid pro quo*.

Rights are moral claims which each individual person has upon other persons and upon all associations of other persons, including in particular the state; and they remain valid whether he is a good man or an evil man, whether he performs his duties or fails to perform them. Duties are obligations morally binding on each person, whatever his situation, whether other men, groups of men, or the state respect his rights or trample upon them. No man can give as an excuse for failure to carry out a duty that others have failed to respect his rights. No man, no group of men, no state, can give as an excuse for depriving an individual person of his inherent rights that he has failed to perform a duty. Duties and rights both derive from the same source, the moral ground of man's nature. But if they are made directly dependent one upon the other, they cease to be rights or duties. Losing their moral autonomy, rights become privileges dispensed to the individual by society or the state, and duties become obediences extorted by power as a payment for privileges.

The *form* that the duties incumbent upon any individual person will take will depend, first, upon the position in life and the endowments of the person concerned and, secondly, upon social circumstances; but the essential content of his duties, always reflecting the moral law, remains the same, whatever his position and capability, whatever the customs of society or the laws of the state. Similarly, the forms in which a man's rights are expressed may vary with time and place and custom, but the content remains the same—the right to live uncoerced by force or fraud in the possession of life, liberty, and property.

The inherent nature of the rights and duties of an individual person, in short, is such that they are not dependent one upon the other. Nor, in any sense, are rights derived from society or the state, or subordinated to duties towards society or the state.

A problem, however, remains—one that can never be finally solved, although the entire structure of the social order and, first of all, the political order, the state, exists primarily as a means to its solution. That problem arises out of the dilemma of virtue and freedom, and out of the corollary contradiction that one man's freedom can be used to inhibit another man's freedom. The refusal by some persons to accept their duties, to obey the moral law, means that the rights of others have no protection from these predators unless they are restrained by force—that is to say, unless *their* freedom is interfered with and *their* rights limited. But since no man is perfect and no one can be depended upon absolutely to fulfill the whole duty of man in letter and spirit, prudential considerations require what the pure philosophical concept of rights cannot brook: that the absolute ideal of the rights of the person must be and will be modified in actual historical existence to the degree necessary to reach the closest possible approximation to that ideal for each individual person.

To say this is not to say that the inherent rights of the human being are—as ideal and as the standard by which actual practice is to be judged—any the less absolute. Nor is it to say that rights are in their essence expedient means towards "social harmony" or the reward dispensed by society or the state for duties fulfilled. Rights, rather, are obligations upon the state to respect the inherent nature of individual human beings and to guarantee to them conditions in which they can live as human beings, that is, in which they can exercise the freedom which is their innate essence. The paradox that to achieve this it is necessary in practice to restrain the freedom of individuals to interfere with other individuals is the reason for the state's existence. And the political order is to be judged, therefore, in terms of its success in dealing with this paradox of social existence, in terms of its preservation of the conditions of freedom.

Political Order and Practical Politics

To give primacy to principle over experience and to insist that freedom is the first criterion of the political order is neither to ignore experience nor to forget that a complex of factors in the minds and lives of men affects the ways in which it is possible at any given time and place to achieve political conditions for the exercise of freedom. Freedom remains the criterion, principle the guide; but the application of principle to circumstances demands a prudential art. The intricate fibers of tradition and civilization, carried in the minds of men from generation to generation, always affect the realization of any general principle. Furthermore, no practical situation can be the direct reflection of a single principle, however important. The compelling, if secondary, claims of other principles, though not decisive to judgment in the political sphere in the way that freedom is, do nevertheless bear upon every concrete political problem. Considering the condition of man as an imperfect being, there are likely to be a number of political orders which are more or less tolerable in terms of freedom (but none of which is perfect), as there are undoubtedly some which are intolerable.

At this point, once again one runs afoul of both the liberal collectivists and the New Conservatives. To the one, such an approach, with its concern for prudence and tradition, is unscientific in the extreme, smelling of obscurantism and the dark unenlightenment of the peasant. To the other, the emphasis on reason and principle is the arch heresy of all Jacobins and liberals, which leads directly to totalitarianism.

The collectivist liberal has no use for anything that is not operationally purposeful. One of his few inheritances from the nineteenth-century liberal is the engineer's approach to political and social matters. Although the twentieth-century collectivist substitutes pragmatic "models" for the rational theory of the older liberal, he is just as eager to use those "models" as tools to transform the world from top to bottom to fit his scientistic preconceptions as was his forebear to build Utopias to match his rational vision. The long-established ways of men, the multifarious modes they have found to mediate between conflicting interests and conflicting principles, and the national and local peculiarities of social orders arising from the history of humankind and its great diversity all must be razed by the builder's demolition engines, ground to powder, to make way for new aseptic constructions that will, with maximum efficiency, cover the social landscape.

The New Conservative, on the other hand, insists, as we have seen, that the application of reason to political and social matters is dangerous in the extreme. To the degree reason is exerted at all, he demands that it be within very narrow limits and in strict subordination to the dictates of tradition. While rational reform is not ruled out for details of the social structure, the very notion of judging an existing society in its totality by rational standards is blasphemy. Prudence, therefore, becomes the master of reason, not its servant. The wisdom that counsels attention to circumstance in the application of reason becomes a blind acceptance of circumstance, which leaves the reason helpless beneath the ponderous weight of what is.

Between the Scylla of abstract application of reason or scientific method (without prudential consideration of circumstance) and the Charybdis of unquestioning reliance on what is (which exalts expedience far above reason), the course to be steered is a difficult one. It is not only that the basic criterion of freedom must be applied to differing historical and cultural circumstances with a different perspective, since the same kind of political order which in one set of historical conditions would represent a large approach to freedom would at another time and place be close to intolerable from the point of view of freedom. Even apart from changing circumstances and varying traditions, there remains the general difficulty, existent at all times and all places, which I have already discussed: the contradiction within freedom itself, the sad fact that any man's freedom can be used, if he so wills, to restrict or destroy another man's freedom. From this there arises an ineluctable imperfection in any political theory or any set of political institutions which takes freedom as its criterion. Completely aside from the emphases or distortions that special interests—personal or group, material or ideal—may introduce, it is this contradiction which makes it impossible for any political order to reflect the pure concept of freedom with crystal clarity. Any such order must find a way whereby one man in his freedom can be restrained from interfering with the freedom of another man, a way which still maintains the protection of freedom to each man to the greatest possible degree. And in so doing, it will depart perforce from abstract purity of principle.

But to stress the impossibility of constructing a Utopia, to insist upon the inherent limitations in the nature of things that inhibit logical perfection in society, is not to resign the function of reason in political thought. Although social and political institutions can never reflect with the perfection of a geometrical image the ideal that a theory based upon the nature of man demands of them, it nevertheless remains true that it is only possible to think and act at the same time morally and intelligently in the political sphere if an ideal standard is constantly kept in view.

It is possible, of course, to act *intelligently* (for example, in a Machiavellian manner), without consideration of such a standard. It is also possible to act *morally* in the political sphere, obeying the imperatives that press upon the individual person acting in a given situation without consideration of the end towards which the political structure should be shaped—and many good and noble men have done so, following their duty where they found it. But insofar as their actions are considered *politically*, they can hardly be said to be acting *intelligently*. And certainly their thinking is not in the strict sense political thinking at all.

That the ideal can never be realized in an imperfect world is no more reason for giving up the effort to move towards it than—to use an analogy from mechanics—the impossibility of ever achieving the perfect frictionless machine is reason to give up the effort to reduce friction to a minimum. Nor, however much contemporary circumstances inhibit an easy or quick achievement of a markedly closer approximation to the ideal, is this a valid objection to the judgment of those circumstances in the light of an ideal end, to the presentation of political theory in that light, or to the demand that political activity should be considered in that light.

Objection to these conclusions can be valid only for one of two reasons. It may deny the truth of the ends posited—that is, it may differ upon the nature of men. Or it may maintain that the nature of the world in which men live is such that it inexorably demands a social and political structure of another sort, irrespective of the demands of principles derived from the nature of men. That is, it may differ upon the nature of men's relationship to their world and conceive of "social laws" as iron laws, as irrelevant to men's effort to realize their being as are the laws of physics.

But once granted that the nature of men is essentially what it has here been maintained to be, and granted that the forms of the political order can be shaped within the broad limitations of existing material circumstance by conscious effort directed towards an end, then the difficulties of achieving an approximation to that end cannot logically be adduced in objection. The kind of order a society has becomes susceptible to the criterion of political theory. Criticism of it becomes, in fact, the reason for existence of political theory and the prime duty of political theorists. The state ceases to be a mystical being to be worshipped or a set of data to be studied behavioristically; it is seen as subject to judgment by criteria drawn from theoretical enquiry, judgment which assesses it in terms of its service to the free being of individual human persons.

5

LEVIATHAN

VIEW OF LEVIATHAN: The State in Theory

The state is not coextensive with the totality of that which it governs; it is a definite group of men, distinct and separate from other men, a group of men possessing the monopoly of legal coercive force. And it remains thus set off, separate, whether it governs with or without the consent of the governed, with or without their participation in the choice of the governors. Even in a democratic polity, the state is not "we," identical with all the people, as is so often claimed; it is "they," those who hold state power. Rarely in political theory is the state thus presented for what it is: a special and limited institution. What is in actuality a specific power is hallowed with the aura of universality. Theory thereby gives sanction to the state's bursting the limits of its proper function—with the ever-present danger of its becoming an all-embracing Leviathan.

The State in Classical Political Philosophy

The origin of the failure to understand that the state is a special and limited institution lies in the history of political philosophy. As a systematic discipline, our political philosophy begins with the Greeks. It is they who established its mode of enquiry and denominated the great questions with which Western political philosophy has been concerned. While in general their approach was so profound as to reach to enduring realities transcending their particular social order, the characteristics of that social order and the form of consciousness of the era necessarily precluded the concept of the state as distinguishable from the aggregate of those under its governance.

In the first place, so far as the social order is concerned, the Greek city-state, the *polis,* was a unity of political government, religious cult, and community association. The opening sentence of Aristotle's *Politics* reads: "Every *polis* [state] is a kind of *koinonia* [communion, community, association]. . . . It is that *koinonia* which is the highest of all and which embraces all the rest, aims at good in a higher degree than any other, and at the highest good."[26] This statement, like the well-known passage in Plato's *Republic*[27] where, beginning the discussion of justice, Socrates posits the state as the individual writ large, shows how thoroughly the concept of the state as an entity coextensive with all citizens and with all their other associations—an entity possessing a moral being of its own—dominated classical political philosophy.

Secondly, and even more compelling to the thought of the Greeks in this respect than their practical circumstances were the limiting forms of their consciousness. The philosophical life of Greece, like the roughly contemporaneous life of Israel, had broken with the immemorial world outlook of the great early civilizations.[28] In these social orders civilization was first born and in them men had lived for most of their civilized existence:

---

26. Aristotle *Politics* 1.1252a.

27. Plato *The Republic* 2.368.

28. For the essential point here made, see the extensive and meticulous scholarly work of Eric Voegelin: *The New Science of Politics* (Chicago: University of Chicago Press, 1952) and *Order and History,* vol. 1, *Israel and Revelation;* vol. 2, *The World of the Polis;* and vol. 3, *Plato and Aristotle* (Baton Rouge: Louisiana

Egypt, Mesopotamia, China (before Lao-Tse and Confucius), India (before Gautama Buddha and Jainism). In these awesomely stable and revolving societies, the ultimate Truth was felt and understood in such identity with the factual presence of civil rule and social being that the judgment of social institutions by the criterion of transcendental truth was inherently impossible. Reality and symbol were so unified that God and King, Heaven and Earth, Truth and Representation, could not in any analytical sense be separated one from another.

Greek philosophical speculation—in Hellas the parallel to the historical-existential prophecy of Israel—burst through this unity of the transcendental and the immanent, a unity in which neither word could have meaning since the universe was a cosmic unity of ultimate reality and present actuality. Between a social order below and a cosmic order above, both Greek and Jew were suddenly able to perceive an immense chasm. In their different ways, each became aware of the difference between what is and what ought to be, between the immanent play of events in the world of actuality and the transcendent source of value from which meaning and judgment are derived. But deep as this revolution in ways of thought was, it stopped short of the stark confrontation of the individual person with the ultimate source of his being. For the Greeks and the Jews political and social institutions ceased to partake, as they had done, of the essence of cosmic truth; but still they—not the individual men who made them up, but they as collectives, the *polis* or "the Chosen People"—were the fundamental moral agents whose action might be judged by transcendent standards. There are, it is true, exceptions in the records we have. There are individuals—an Abraham at the sacrifice of Isaac, a Socrates drinking the hemlock—who for a moment stand at the center of the moral drama. But Abraham

State University Press, 1956, 1957, 1957). The interpretation and development of the point, however, is my own; for it he is in no way responsible.

is in the end an epitome of the Chosen People; and Socrates, as he has come down to us, is the representative of the *polis* that ought to be. He has been sentimentalized as a champion of individual liberty, standing against the state. But even the most casual unprejudiced reading of the *Apology* and the *Crito*—to say nothing of the *Republic*—will show that he stood not as champion of the person, but as the prophet of the righteous *polis* against the bad *polis*. The Socrates who drank the hemlock is the same Socrates who discoursed in the *Republic;* and it is the *Republic,* in which men are but parts of an organic state, that represents the inner Hellenic feeling about the matter of political theory. The less absolute images of the political process presented in Plato's *Laws* or in Aristotle's *Politics* are imbued with the same spirit, however they may differ from the *Republic* in emphasis.

This inability to free themselves from the *polis* experienced as an organic being, of which individual men are but cells, was an omnipresent limit upon the genius of the Greeks in political-theoretical speculation. Their thought could only break outside its bounds in occasional lofty insights of the greatest of the Greek philosophers. But in their general system these forms of consciousness were never overcome. It is the measure of their genius that their analytical ability still holds our political theory in thrall, despite all that has occurred since, philosophically and theologically, to free the person from the bonds of existence as a cell in an organic state-community.

The Christian Doctrine of the Person

Between the Hellenic world and ours lies a second great revolution in human consciousness. The Incarnation and the Christian doctrine of the person that flows from it break finally and forever the unity of cosmos and person. The offer of Grace through the penetration of the Divine into the immanent world overcomes the lonely horror implicit in a clear and sharp separation between the world and the transcendent—a horror which had inhibited the mind from accepting such a separation and thus driven it back again and again to the cosmological fleshpots of Egypt. God's sacrifice in love bridged that gulf and made it possible for men to face each his indissoluble identity and accept its responsibilities. It now becomes clear not just that there is a dichotomy between transcendent truth and immanent actuality (the new understanding of Greece and Israel), but that only the person can be the earthly pole of the discharge between the transcendent and the immanent. The sanctity is drained out of all institutions of an earthly nature. For no community, no state, no association—only persons, individual human beings—can receive the beatific vision or be redeemed by the divine sacrifice of love.

I have said "is"—that the sanctity of institutions *is* drained out. I should have said "should be" drained out. It would be, if our theoretical thinking about political matters reached the highest level made possible by the Christian vision of the human drama. In fact, however, at this essential point—the primacy of the individual person in political thought and political practice—a portentous distortion occurs. So influenced are we by the Greek origins of our thinking about political matters that the best of our political theory remains imprisoned within their forms of consciousness. A political theory raised to the height that the Christian sense of the value of the person makes possible has not been developed.

The desanctification of the state is epitomized in the commandment *Render therefore unto Caesar the things which be Caesar's, and unto God the things which be God's.* Unhappily, this has been too often understood either as an ascetic counsel to the godly man to suffer what earthly powers bring to bear upon him and to ignore the problems of civil society, or as a sanctification of the state as possessing in the area of earthly matters a divine authority. But the plain meaning would seem to be to understand the difference between the things of God and the things of Caesar and to think and act accordingly, neither to turn one's back upon the world nor on the other hand to consider the political institutions that from time to time well or ill serve human needs as in any sense themselves divine.

If this precept so understood is explicitly held in mind, the primacy of the person looms so large that the secondary and derivative character of the state as a necessary, but limited, earthly institution, and not more, becomes sharply apparent. The state ceases to be seen as an institution universal and coextensive with the sum of human relations that is called society. It becomes possible for political theory to break out of the bonds imposed on it by the men of genius who created it, to overcome the limits of the conditions of the Greek consciousness, and to attain the deeper understanding accessible to it on the basis of the Western doctrine of the person.

Utopians of Babel

These possibilities have not been realized. Political theory is still obfuscated by a fascination with the state considered as an entity to which value attaches over and above that which it derives from individual human beings. That this is so is, of course, due not only to the heritage of classical political theory.

From the beginnings of Western civilization, there have been undertones of another kind of thought, radically different from either the Classical or the Christian, about man and his social development. Utopians, in the dream of a this-worldly paradise, unwilling to accept as an innate aspect of existence the imperfection of men and seeing in political power the engine for the creation of a world in their own image of perfection, have glorified and divinized the state—although for different, almost for opposite, reasons than the followers of classical political theory. During the past few centuries these undertones have swelled till they have become the prevailing component of Western thought.

The origins of this outlook are obscure, but they must go back to at least the second millennium B.C. The myth of the Tower of Babel, like the historical record of the reign of the Pharaoh Akhenaton, who attempted to reconstruct Egyptian society in a single generation, testifies to so early an existence of the belief that men can create a perfect world. It exists in the Hellenic world side by side with the dominant classical political theory (among, for example, the Pythagoreans and the neo-Platonists), and it persists in many of the Gnostic sects, through whom undoubtedly it was transmitted to Western civilization. Always since, it has been endemic as an underground aspect of Western thought, appearing now and again in the Utopianism and millenarianism of some medieval heresies, until it rises fully to the surface in two forms almost simultaneously: in the passionate revolutionism of Anabaptist and Puritan and in the vision of knowledge as power, symbolized by the legend of Faust and soberly inculcated in the essays of Lord Bacon. In the colossal explosion of the French Revolution, the two forms came together. The *philosophes* of the Enlightenment are, equally with men of passion like Rousseau and St.-Just, creators of that cataclysm and of the deification of nation and state following from it. The dominant ideologies of the twentieth century—Communism, Fascism, socialism, and that amalgam of positivism, pragmatism, and welfarism which is the ideology of the collectivist liberals—are the latest forms taken by this Utopian attitude.

Those who look on existence in this way, who conceive that the nature of men can be changed to meet the specifications of a design of earthly perfection, need perforce some mechanism through which to act. That mechanism must be one suited to the exercise of power by men who are certain that they, and they alone, understand what must be done and who are fired by the mission to force their understanding upon the great mass of other men who do not understand. The mechanism stands ready to hand. The state, which is the sole universally accepted repository of force, need only be captured, and that force extended beyond its natural purposes.

The state, therefore, becomes the great engine of social transformation. Every revolutionary movement of the last two centuries—however much it may have begun by radical criticism of the state it found in being—ends by deifying the state it has captured and theologizing the concept of the state. Jacobinism, Marxism, Fascism, collectivist liberalism, each in its own way has joined intellectually and emotionally in the deification of the state, and each in its own way has contributed to that immense growth in the power of the state which is the effective condition of totalitarianism.

The State as Mystery

From this heritage the collectivist-liberal attitude towards the state is derived. Against it classical political theory is helpless, because classical political theory shares with it an apotheosis of the state. But it is upon classical political theory that the New Conservative view of the state is founded. This is not to say that there is not an important difference between the collectivist liberals and the New Conservatives—as wide a one as there is between the Utopian and the classical theories of which they are respectively the heirs. The classical political outlook was deeply moral; its identification of state and society and the placing of state-society as an independent entity taking precedence over the person were the results of circumstances, a limitation of vision, not the destruction of an achieved understanding. Utopianism, on the other hand, is the deliberate rejection of an existing understanding of the nature of the person for the sake of a hubristic determination to dominate reality, to make it over in the image of the human makers.

Wide though this difference is, however, the collectivist liberal and the New Conservative are agreed in refusing to accept the state as an institution which is the expression of the power of a specific group of men, power which can only be justified in terms of a specific function. Unless the state is thus conceived, as an institution of specific function, composed of specific men in given relations, it is not only impossible to subject it to value criteria derived from the nature of the human person; it also seems to become impossible even to recognize the actuality of states as they are. It seems to become necessary to insist that they are one with the citizens they govern in a holistic unity. The simple and obvious differentiation between the governed and the governors (apparent every time an arrest is made, a tax is collected, or a judgment enforced) disappears. The state becomes "all of us" and more than any collection of each of us—an entity surcharged with value.

The development of democracy has made critical recognition of the dichotomy between the state and those whom the state governs particularly difficult. In a monarchy or an aristocracy or an oligarchy, or in such a combination of the three forms as England exhibited in the eighteenth century, or in that combination of aristocracy, democracy, and elective monarchy that the United States exhibited in its early days, the dogma of the state as coextensive with the being of all the persons living under it was more easily controverted than in a social order that men think of as democratic. But the reality is fundamentally the same, whether the political order is democratic or not. Those who possess the power of the state possess it exclusively and over against the rest of society, whether their power is confirmed by hereditary right, landed property, wealth, or the democratic ballot.

In the last case, it is much more difficult to confute the fallacy which confuses the *power to pass upon who shall govern* with the *power to govern*. Even if the institutional structure of the state did not, as in fact it does, create a continuity among the holders of power irrespective of the outcome of party politics, even if annual elections changed the governors constantly and men were forbidden to succeed themselves in power, the essential separation of the state from the rest of social existence would still remain. For the time that they were in power, the governors would still be governors. The state would still be raised out of, and exist over against, the rest of society.

To grasp this elemental distinction is the first condition of a theory of the state. If the state remains in the realm of mystery, which is proper not to institutions but to God and the final nature of men, it cannot in any serious sense be brought under theoretical consideration on a political level, for its own being is then the only possible criterion of judgment. Hegel has been much castigated in late years for his glorification of the state as the spirit of God in the world, but he only carried to a logical conclusion what our most accepted political theory implies in a more clouded way.

A Critical Theory of the State

But if the state is regarded as an institution critically delimitable and serving a given function in the affairs of men, it can then be brought under criteria derived from higher philosophical consideration. It can be considered as all other institutions are considered. An ideal image of what it should be can be projected; given states can be judged by the criteria by which all human institutions should be judged: their adequacy in their own sphere to the achievement of the best possible circumstances in which human beings may work out their destiny. From the primary problem of politics, the tension of freedom and order, we have drawn the principles for judgment of that adequacy: those principles demand a state capable of maintaining order while at the same time guaranteeing to each person in its area of government the maximum liberty possible to him short of his interference with the liberty of other persons.

Anarchists maintain that this goal can be best achieved without any state whatsoever; and if their argument were valid, the best state would be no state at all. But, to return for a moment to a previous point in this discussion, brute facts invalidate their thesis. The nature of men and of freedom is such that some men may use their freedom to interfere with the freedom of others, to impose upon them with violence. In a stateless society, the only answer to such conduct is to return violence with violence, and this, we can be sure, would end in a Hobbesian "war of all against all." Some form of order is a human necessity. Without it, freedom itself is impossible. The state—that is, an institution recognized as the repository of legitimate violence to inhibit one man in his freedom from destroying another man's freedom—is therefore an institution called into being by the very nature of men's existence. It is a necessary and natural institution—so long as it fulfills its function and does not use its power for purposes extraneous to that function.

Furthermore, even were men not so constituted that some will always use their freedom in such a way as to interfere with the freedom of other men, even were the state not therefore necessary to protect the rights of individual persons against wrongful interference, there would still exist another problem that would make the state necessary. This is the perennial problem of the social order, the conflict of rights with rights. That conflict has always required the existence of a recognized source of justice, possessing a monopoly of rightful force by which to impose its judgment on individuals and groups of individuals. Were there no institution of judgment available to decide the conflict of rights with rights, the only recourse at the margin would be recourse to violence in the name of one right against a clashing right.

The state therefore has two natural functions, functions essential to the existence of any peaceful, ordered society: to protect the rights of citizens against violent or fraudulent assault and to judge in conflicts of right with right. It has a further third function, which is another aspect of the first, that is, to protect its citizens from assault by foreign powers. These three functions are expressed by three powers: the police power, which protects the citizen against domestic violence; the military power, which protects the citizen against violence from abroad; and the courts of law, which judge between rights and rights, as well as sharing with the police power the protection of the citizen against domestic violence. The first two of these powers, the police and the military, coincide with the executive functions of government; the courts, with the judicial function; and the legislature enacts the laws (upon generally accepted fundamental concepts of morality) which the executive and the judiciary enforce. Insofar as the state fulfills these functions—the protection of citizens against violence, domestic and foreign, and the administration of justice, it plays a necessary role. To this degree, and within these limits, it is not possible to conceive of ordered human existence without the state. These functions must be fulfilled, and the state is defined in its essence as the institution which fulfills them.

But since this institution must possess a monopoly of legal physical force, to give to it in addition any further power is fraught with danger; that monopoly gives to the state so much power that its natural functions should be its maximum functions. Any activity not absolutely vital to the operation of the state in its functional capacity can only add further power to what is always a dangerous, if necessary, measure of power. And even that power will have to be hedged around and divided among a number of more or less independent centers if the state is not to become a danger to liberty. Those living under the state, to which they have yielded up the monopoly of legitimate armed force, cannot afford to yield it an iota more of control over their lives. When the state enters the economic sphere, when the state makes positive rules as to how men shall live that go beyond the preservation of the essential conditions of a free order, when the state takes upon itself the education of children or insurance against the hazards of life—with each of these steps its monopoly of force in the form of violence is fortified by control of economic, social, and ideological life. Step by step it amasses the decisive control of society. Each step makes the next one easier, and each step makes it harder to reverse the process. The state, from a natural and necessary institution in the social order, becomes a Leviathan, amassing to itself a decisive power that can only end in the destruction of the liberty of its citizens.

Not least of the conditions essential if the state is to be prevented from becoming such a Leviathan is the theoretical concept of the state that prevails. If it is a concept which is in accord with the nature of man, then the actual state will be judged by that concept and men will be impelled to act to hold the state within bounds. The image of the state projected in this book is, of course, an ideal. No historic state has ever fully reflected it, and by the nature of things it is impossible that any future state will fully do so. There is in power an impulsion to more power, which can only be limited by countermeasures. The state will always tend to move beyond its natural bounds, and the men who hold its power will always attempt to gain more power. But the need for a constant struggle to limit the state does not weaken the validity of the concept of a state limited to its natural function, as the theoretical standard by which to judge the practice and the claims of every historical state. Indeed, without such a concept, without such an ideal image, it would be impossible to combat that integral movement of power towards more power that must be combated if freedom is to be preserved in an ordered society.

In the practical political thinking and action that go into the foundation and maintenance of a political order, the establishment of a just balance, which limits government to its legitimate functions while allowing it strength enough to carry out those functions effectively, is a most difficult problem. It requires the combination of a firm hold upon principle with a prudential understanding of the application of principle to changing and varied human situations. An extreme instance of this problem is the conflict between the demands of the state for the power to carry out its legitimate functions in time of war and the danger that such crises will create state power of a permanent kind that goes beyond those legitimate functions. Though this is an extreme instance, practical problems of the same sort, if of less urgency, arise constantly in the year-to-year life of any people. I do not mean to minimize the immense difficulties of solving them; but they can be solved, at least approximately, by a continuing process of prudential application of theoretical principles to changing circumstances.

LEVIATHAN ENLARGED:
The Liberal-Collectivist State

The dominant motif of political thought today is the denial of a principled theory of politics based on philosophical consideration of the nature of man. The state is to be understood not by establishing what it ought to be and criticizing its actuality in terms of what it ought to be, but by a minute and detailed study of the functioning of states as they happen to be. And those happenings are interpreted as no more or less than a struggle for power and gain. In the now well-worn words of Harold D. Lasswell, a Nestor of American "political science," the study of politics is the study of "who gets what, when, how."

Proponents and practitioners of this "political science," although they are united in their scorn for political *philosophy* (which, in Professor Lasswell's words, has significance only because it "justifies preferences"), strangely enough almost unanimously share a single well-defined set of axiomatic beliefs, upon which they act and which controls their "scientific" work. The human mind cannot in fact function without philosophical principles, whether they are consciously arrived at and held or unconsciously and uncritically taken for granted. It is therefore no wonder that among contemporary liberals the relativist methodology, which denies the very existence of principles, is found in symbiosis with hard-bitten collectivist principles. These latter are not proclaimed as principles, it is true; they are simply assumed as the natural truth at which all objective investigation will arrive. Arrive, indeed, our scientists do—"value free," feverishly collecting data, "evaluating" those collections, and, at the end of the process, neatly delivering the conclusions which they held to begin with. These conclusions are the credo of collectivist liberals in the political sphere, as their peculiar mixture of historical determinism with moral and methodological relativism is in the philosophical sphere.

"People," State, Bureaucratic Elite

Since for a century or more it has been possible to proclaim that God—and with Him the transcendental foundation of value—is dead, all value (the word is retained in decent, or in opportunist, deference to the prejudices of men) can be derived only from the facts of human existence. These facts disclose to us a world in which "the people" nominally, the state in their name, and the manipulators of "the people" in reality control political happenings.

These three elements, the "people," the state which rules in their name, and the bureaucratic elites which in effect control the state, are the cardinal terms upon which the entire structure of contemporary liberal political science is erected. The state is the middle term by which the sanction of "the people," the ultimate authority in the liberal-collectivist cosmology, is transmitted to the elite which rules in its name. This paradigm of the social order is projected not only logically—to the degree that the atomized empiricisms of the "social-scientific method" allow of a coherent logic—but also rhetorically. The

rhetorical identification of the state with the people, together
with the rhetorical identification of the executive with the state
and the exaltation of the expert over the political man, leads
directly to the legitimization of the bureaucracy.

This bureaucracy is not composed simply of government
civil servants, although it is in their hands that decisive operative power rests. It is rather a composite of several groups with
different functional positions and some different parochial interests, but with an essential unity of ideological outlook and
underlying interest that becomes greater year by year. It includes, in addition to the bureaucracy of the government, the
opinion moulders of the mass-communications industry, the
salaried manageriat,[29] both of industry and the trade unions—
and the decisive sections of the academic personnel of the major universities, where for the past fifty years the ideology of
this entire composite elite has been formed.

It is not accidental that the positivist-pragmatist ideology of
these fifty years finds its end point in the establishment of its
ideologists as a bureaucracy, backed directly and indirectly by
the power of the state. The philosophical essence of the whole
intellectual movement of the century has been the concept of
control, of power—as surely in collectivist liberalism as in
Marxism. The foundation of this kind of power in political and
social affairs must necessarily be the state, whether that power
is exerted directly, as under totalitarian circumstances, or indirectly, as in the circumstances of a welfarist collectivism of the
type which has been steadily developing in the United States
since 1932. The existence of truly independent centers of
power, not subject to the state and uncorrelated by the state,
forecloses success for an ideological attitude that sees its concepts as valid only as they become pragmatically operative: so
many engineering principles, they have no meaning except as
they are given reality in material activity. The existence of un-

29. "Manageriat" is, I know, a barbarous and an ugly coinage—but apt,
because it reflects a barbarous and an ugly reality.

trammeled independent centers of power in society is as frustrating to the holders of such a philosophy as the existence of untrammeled centers of direction in a building crew would be to a construction engineer. Indeed, images like this are often used by the collectivists as arguments in favor of their social and political programs. And such arguments would be compelling, if the building gang were an apt simile for the human race and if the destiny of men were, simply and exhaustively, to build, to make, to construct.

From the need to vindicate this view of man arises the other side of the liberal-collectivist position, an aspect of it which is prior both logically and in time: the relativist attack upon the image of man as an autonomous center of outgoing will. In place of that image, the relativist image is one of man as the resultant of physical and biological vectors, ascertainable and manipulable by any bright engineer. Men cease to be independent centers of will, free to act. They become either cells in a social organism whose will they reflect or an inchoate collection of atoms that must be directed and brought into pattern as History or Progress or Science demands. The collectivist liberal and the Marxist plump for the latter alternative: men are atoms and must be organized in the proper pattern. The god who breathes through the collectivist liberal as he fulfills the mission of organization and direction is a hybrid of Science and Progress; the god who breathes through the Marxist fulfilling the same mission is a hybrid of History, Progress, and Science. The alternative solution when the autonomy of men is denied—the apotheosis of Society as an organism with men as its cells—is the one towards which New Conservative thought tends; but of that, more later.

To return to the collectivist liberals: if men are atoms to be arranged as engineering principles dictate, political power is the only force available to arrange them. It is here that the state becomes the decisive institution. It can be used directly and brutally, as in the Bolshevik revolution, or indirectly and subtly, as in the Roosevelt revolution. It is undoubtedly pleasanter to live under the conditions brought about by the latter revolution, and it is much more possible to reserve the trend; but in terms of social and political reality, the aims of the two revolutions are parallel. Each is directed towards bringing into power an elite dedicated to the principled suppression of the freedom of men as innate centers of will in order to remake the world in the image of its particular operational blueprint.

The Quadripartite Bureaucracy[30]

If it should seem that I am exaggerating the significance of state power as the foundation of the position of the decisive elites, consider the actual situation. Fifty or seventy-five years ago, of the four divisions of the ruling bureaucracy, not one had any direct impact upon the lives and fortunes of the citizens of the United States.

a. The Government Bureaucracy

The government bureaucracy hardly existed; insofar as government directly affected the lives of citizens (and that, except in time of war, was to a very small degree indeed), it was government as expressed in elected officials and legislatures, primarily those of the several states and municipalities. Taxes and regulations were almost entirely in the hands of the municipal subdivisions; a Whisky Rebellion in 1794 or a Pullman strike in 1894 might bring the power of the federal government into direct contact with the citizen, but, except in time of war, this was extremely rare. The creation of the government bureaucracy as we know it today has taken place in the last few decades.

30. I owe to Willmoore Kendall the beginnings of my understanding of this phenomenon, to which he pointed in unpublished lectures that I have had the privilege of reading and which I have had the opportunity of discussing with him at length in private conversation.

b. The Trade-Union and Corporation Bureaucracy

The salaried manageriat of the great trade unions and the great corporations is almost entirely a creation of the years since 1932. Trade unions were not a power capable of imping-ing upon national life until they were called into existence as a major force by the Roosevelt administration, using Section 7-A of the NRA and the Wagner Labor Relations Act. The control of the corporations by a salaried manageriat that differs less and less day by day from the salaried manageriat which rules the trade unions is also a recent development. These "organi-zation men" have succeeded to much of the power of the en-trepreneurial capitalists, who have been undermined as a decisive class in the community by the taxation policies, the regulatory policies, the managed inflation, and the redistribu-tive welfare economics inaugurated by the New Deal and car-ried forward by every administration since, Democratic or Republican. They have no significant personal ownership of the industrial power they control, simply administering vast masses of capital in the name of stockholders, as government bureaucrats administer the state in the name of "the people." The power is theirs, but it is a form of power similar to that of the government bureaucrat or the trade-union bureaucrat; and it attracts and creates a similar human type, with similar interests and similar functions.

c. The Mass-Communications Bureaucracy

The mass-communications bureaucracy is less directly and less obviously the creation of the state. But its immense power and decisive position would never have been achieved except for conditions traceable to the collectivist development of the state. The techniques with which that bureaucracy operates are directed towards what one of their number has called "the en-gineering of consent." The key word in that phrase is "engineering"; and this word implies psychological modes of persuasion directed towards the common denominator of a mass public, not the rational and rhetorical persuasion of a critical and highly individualized public. These "persuaders" had their origins in private salesmanship and "publicity," but their emergence and success as a powerful bureaucracy influencing public policy is a comparatively new phenomenon. It only became possible with the substitution of the mass, the undifferentiated and inarticulate "people," for an independent and differentiated middle class[31] as the public towards which appeals on social and political questions are directed.

An independent middle class does not mean high-salaried technologists, professionals, and managers, economically dependent upon conformity to the norms of the social machine. It does not mean William L. Whyte's "organization man," no matter how wealthy or how powerful he may be. It means literal independence, economic independence, for a sufficient number of persons, with fortunes ranging from what used to be called a modest competence upwards, to provide a stable center to the social order—whether this independence arises from personal ownership and management of enterprise or from income derived from land or investment. This is the public opinion which has passed judgment upon the claims of the powerful and the persuasive in all free modern societies.

The elimination of this independent, informed, and critical court of final appeal and its replacement by an undifferentiated mass subject to the emotions of the mob have been the necessary prelude to the establishment of every despotism

31. John Stuart Mill thoroughly understood the decisive role of such a public, the role of the middle class in his time, in making a free social order possible. He went far astray, however, under the influence of a doctrinaire democratism when he projected that role to the whole of the population, assuming that wholesale education could create the same qualities in tens of millions of dependent men that a select education and the influence of continuing families had created in tens of thousands of independent men.

since the devotees of Rousseau's General Will and St.-Just's Nation, invoking the Terror against the Girondins, made the mob of Paris the arbiter of France's destinies. It is possible in the span of a generation or two to eliminate such a middle class without terror or physical liquidation. Inheritance taxes, which eat away the substance of families who concern themselves not with the accumulation of money, but with carrying forward and developing the tradition of the civilization; a steeply graduated progressive income tax, which almost entirely inhibits the possibility of establishing an estate and founding a family free from the external pressures of society: these will in the space of a few decades destroy all independence, except that of a few very wealthy families. It is this process, which we have witnessed during the past thirty years, that has largely destroyed the classes which traditionally represented decisive public opinion, replacing them with the pliable mass public of today. Harry Hopkins's "tax, tax, tax; spend, spend, spend; elect, elect, elect" is—a little expanded—an elegant syllogistic exposition of the process: tax to destroy the independent; spend to create the dependent; from the destruction of the one and the elevation of the other, maintain the power of the bureaucratic elite.

The mass-communications bureaucracy is a necessary link in this process. It could never have come into existence without the destruction of the independent position of the middle class; and its positive function is to "engineer the consent" of the engineerable, manipulable mass. It performs the function of creating agreement, which is indispensable to the well-being of the collectivist state and the composite elite which operates through it.

d. The Academic Bureaucracy

The academic bureaucracy—as a bureaucracy, in contradistinction to a calling, a collegium of scholars—is a creation of developing collectivism; and that act of creation has also taken place in comparatively recent years. A long history of ideological development, it is true, prepared the way for this transformation of the scholar into the bureaucrat. After the change in attitude of intellectuals that set in at the Renaissance, signalized by Francis Bacon's words, "knowledge is power," it could only have been a matter of time before what was believed theoretically was expressed in practice. If knowledge is no longer conceived as the search for and the acceptance of truth—an occupation parallel to the occupation of the artist and the occupation of the saint—but as the acquisition of power to control and manipulate nature and man, it logically follows that an attempt will be made to realize that conception in the political sphere. The immense successes of the physical scientists in controlling and manipulating nature perhaps could be paralleled by a reconstruction of society, in which the state would play the role in transforming men that mechanical and industrial power had played in the harnessing of natural forces.

This battening urge for power on the part of the intellectuals—and, in the first instance, the intellectuals of the academy who create the forms of thought of the intellectuals of every sphere in each new generation—is the efficient cause behind the revolution of the twentieth century, whether its form has been Communist, socialist, "nationalist," or welfarist-liberal. It was only with the early years of this century—in the atmosphere of Progressivism and the New Freedom—that the idea that problems of statecraft and political power are in any special sense the concern of the scholar, of the professor, began to develop in this country; but once the idea took root, its effects were tremendous. It would be hard to underestimate the influence of the teaching in the great American universities, of the writing of members of the academy in such journals as the *Nation* and the *New Republic*, in preparing the way for that revolutionary transformation of the American state, the New Deal. And since the success of that revolution, men of the academy have occupied hundreds of prominent positions in the bureaucracy it produced.

The state, however, is a recalcitrant instrument for the academic planners. Power attracts men who are natively attuned to the ring of power and such men inevitably succeed in getting and keeping their hands on the levers of power. Using the academic adventurers only for their services in justifying and preparing the way for the aggrandizement of the power of the state, they realize in a rough political manner the power concepts of the collectivist theories while reducing the theoreticians themselves to the role of an auxiliary bureaucracy, well taken care of if it minds its manners, but powerless to initiate and far from the centers of control.

The natural history of this process is observable throughout the world. In the United States, where what has happened has been less dramatic (no "self-criticism," no blood purges, no intellectual and cultural "lines" handed down from political heights), it has nevertheless run a similar course. In the rapturous springtime of the early Brain Trust, it seemed that the dreams of a generation of academic planners were being realized. The disillusionments with political reality of the academic participants of that day can be read in memoir after memoir—all variations on the theme of The Dream We Lost.[32]

The academic bureaucracy in its present form plays a significant role in the complex of bureaucracies which is given its life blood in the form of money and prestige by a Leviathan of state power that directly controls one-third of the national income and in a diffuse manner controls the general direction of social movement. But it is far from being that direct source of initiative and conscious direction, that brotherhood of

32. One or two of the paladins of 1932—for example, Raymond Moley—have carried their analysis further and to fundamentals and have reached a position critical of the entire philosophical outlook with which they set out on the adventure. But most of the witnesses show a complete unawareness of what hit them. One of the most illuminating of these memoirs—because the author retains a naive and touching personal faith in FDR—is Rexford G. Tugwell's *The Democratic Roosevelt* (New York: Doubleday, 1957).

engineer-philosopher kings, the vision of which stirred the heartstrings of the generation of Dewey and Veblen. The dream of a society hygienically cleansed of the "irrational," the divergent, the contingent, the merely mysterious, may well be on the way to fulfillment; but it is not being achieved, as they dreamt, under their direct control. Not only has the dream failed to come true, but, in the striving for its realization, the ancient and honorable function of scholar and teacher has lost the glorious independence of a vocation dedicated to the pursuit and propagation of truth. The scholar has been reduced to a position of bureaucratic interdependence that in a happier age he would have scorned as the condition of clerks and functionaries.

This is the common fate of all ideologues who preach the virtue of massive and pervasive social power. By the creation of the immense and complex institutional forms necessary for centralized control, the projector becomes the victim of his own project. The scholar becomes the committeeman in a multi-million-dollar, foundation-financed "team" research project, or a cog in a government department; the artist, the writer, is bound to the feverish pace of the mass-communications industry. They have exchanged the independence of thought and action which is the proper activity of a free being for a minute share in the power of an immense machine.

This swallowing up of separate and individual energies in the coordinate functioning of a multiplex bureaucratic society could never have taken place without the bursting of its natural bounds by the state, as the aggrandizement of the power of the state would not have been possible without the floriation of bureaucratic social modes. And neither of these developments could have taken place without the triumph of the collectivist political theories upon which both have been based. Likewise, without their dominance, the destruction of differentiation among human beings and the creation of undifferentiated masses, "the people," (a process still not complete in the

United States, although far advanced under the impact of income and inheritance taxes, inflation, public education, and the indoctrination of equalitarian dogmas) would have been impossible. That among the bureaucratized leaders of society, the major share of direct power rests with those who most clearly understand that in such a society power is an end, not a means, does not minimize the importance of the composite bureaucracy as a whole in controlling the state and manipulating the people.

Is There a Liberal-Collectivist Theory of the State?

These three elements—the state, "the people," and the bureaucratic elite—are the constituents of the "model" (to use their own language), on the basis of which the liberal-collectivist political scientists work. It is from observation of their manipulations of these elements that their theory of the state can be deduced. It might be asked why it is necessary to deduce their theory of the state, rather than go to their writings and establish their theory directly. The fact of the matter is that, except in the writings of the openly or covertly Marxist political scientists, no explicit theory of the state can be found among them. Nor is this astonishing in view of the conditions under which political matters are studied today—conditions I have discussed in previous chapters.

The positivist and scientistic atmosphere, in which ends are exiled from consideration, precludes the study of the state or of any institution on a theoretical basis. Operational studies; comparative discourses upon the functioning of different states; historical discursions on the development of states; elaborate empirical collections of "behavioral" data; analyses of the functioning of power, in the spirit of Thrasymachus and Machiavelli—these are the products of the political scientists of the day, and of their colleagues, the sociologists, the social psychologists, and the nontheoretical economists, to whom what once were integral aspects of political philosophy have been farmed out. In the universities and the scholarly journals, when political philosophy is discussed, it is only by historians. The political theories of Aristotle or Rousseau or Mill, like Magdalenian stone axes, are archaeologically interesting, but one would no more think of devoting one's self to the *pursuit* of theoretical understanding than to the making of stone axes.

Still, since the universe and human beings are as they are, it is not possible to think or act without being subject to the determining forms of some theoretical position, whether it is consciously and formally recognized or not. There *is* a liberal-collectivist theory of the state, which pervades contemporary political thought and action. Because it does exist but is not put forth in explicit form, it is necessary to deduce its tenets. This needs to be done because even when it is recognized that something of a coherent theory underlies the pragmatic statements of collectivist liberalism, its theory of the state is usually equated either with the Marxist theory of the state or with that of nineteenth-century liberalism—depending upon the predilections of the critic. The Protean character of liberal-collectivist pronouncements can perhaps explain so opposite a pair of identifications. But both of these characterizations betray the lack of a serious effort to come to grips with the substance. There can be no doubt that similarities do exist between the liberal-collectivist theory of the state and the Marxist theory; it could not be otherwise when both are associated with collectivist theories of society and the economy. Likewise, a great many of the formal verbalisms of liberal-collectivist thought on political matters seem very close to some formulations of nineteenth-century individualist liberalism. Particularly when the intellectual bureaucracy, in the course of the struggle to control the state, comes into conflict with the efforts of legislative bodies to retain their Constitutional control over public policy, they assume the role of a mere accidental conglomeration of individuals oppressed by state power, which is identified, for the purpose of the drama, with the legislature. Then the liberal collectivist borrows almost verbatim the language of John Stuart Mill—as, for example, in the current discussion of the powers of investigating committees of the Congress.

Nor can it really be said, as is sometimes maintained, that the contradiction between the use of nineteenth-century liberal language for certain purposes and the congruence of many liberal-collectivist propositions to those of Marxism betrays an incoherent eclecticism. It is understandable how that conclusion can be reached, if one considers only the surface aspect, but nevertheless, as I shall show, there does exist a specific liberal-collectivist theory of the state.

"The General Will": Justification of Collectivist Power

Like all twentieth-century theories of the state, the liberal-collectivist theory is a variation on the Rousseauian concept of the state as the embodiment of the General Will. To understand how this concept has been able to be used in one way or another by all the revolutionists of the twentieth century—Communist, Fascist, nationalist, and welfarist—some peculiarities of its structure must be noted. The General Will is not the will of all, or the will of a majority, or the consensus of the interacting wills of groups and individuals, but the Will which all would have if they knew what was really good for them. Rousseau neither takes the positivist position that whatever power wants it will get, and that this is therefore right; nor, on the other hand, does he admit that there exist objective values which are in their essence right and which should therefore be the ends of political order. Rather, the theory of the General Will in a curious way combines positivist glorification of power with the appearance of a value-based justification of that power.

The pure positivist position is obvious for what it is. Its only defense against a value-based politics is power itself; and since, in the long run, even in the middle run, men inevitably seek justification for action in some end towards which it moves, a pure positivist theory of politics could never have wielded influence very far beyond the confines of the study. The theory of the General Will overcomes this practical weakness. Rousseau discarded the heritage of the Christian West and attempted to reinstitute, by an act of intellectual will, the instinctive Greek identification of the good with the state regarded as a corporate body of the citizenry. What was natural to the Greeks, although it was a concept from which their best spirits strove mightily to break away, Rousseau strove mightily to reestablish as truth, against every instinct of Western civilization. Thus he became the presiding genius of the two-hundred-year crisis of the West, in the most frenetic stage of which we live today. He could not, of course, reinstitute Greek consciousness. The corporate sense of the Greeks, which made it possible for Aristotle to say that man is a political animal—an animal of the *polis*—no longer existed in a civilization which regards each individual man, not as an animal whose being rests in the state, but as a person whose being takes meaning from free personal choice of good and evil, a choice dictated by no institution.

This concept of free personal choice affects everyone in the West, even those who seem to have broken most sharply with the theological and philosophical sources from which it springs. Western man regards himself as the center of his own earthly existence. If God and transcendent value no longer serve as goals and guides in the free exercise of his choice, no corporate earthly deity can be re-created from a past civilization to play for him the ego-absorbing function that the *polis* did for the Greek spirit. His consciousness, free and without focus, retains the Western apprehension of person, but its energy, with the inner discipline of its originating world-view gone, acts destructively, like a powerful engine run amok, upon whatever crosses his path. Therefore Rousseau's attempted re-creation of the *polis* in the form of the General Will could not re-create the classical principles of political order which had been destroyed by the attack of Machiavelli and Hobbes on value-based political theory. Rather, the concept of the deified will of the people furnished a quasi-moral justification without specific moral content, ready to be taken hold of by any "elite." Filled with whatever ideological content social circumstances and ideological predilections suggested to them, it was a tool well-adapted to be used, first to raise themselves to power, then to destroy their enemies, and finally to gain consent from the governed. These goals, particularly the last, could never have been reached under the aegis of the naked positivist glorification of power. The theory of the General Will in its various manifestations provided the necessary appearance of moral justification.

The empty abstraction whereby the General Will was identified neither with the particular will of individuals nor of groups nor even of a majority, but with an assumed underlying real will of the totality, enabled each elite in turn to fill out the lineaments of the totality whose will was holy, in such a manner that this will became what the elite wished it to be. Consent was gained and moral rectitude affirmed by an identification of the totality with those whose consent was to be secured. The *Volk* of the Nazis, the proletariat of the Communists, are but manifestations of this totality whose will is the General Will, lay figures draped out to gain the consent of the masses. These figures are presented as if they were indeed the very image of the masses, but in reality they are only representations of the will of the elite: the will of the Communist Party is the true will of the proletariat; the will of the *Führer* is the true will of the German *Volk*. (This is not simple hypocrisy. The leading Communist, the leading Nazi, deeply believes that he does embody the true will of the people, as the Jacobin leaders of the Convention, Rousseau's immediate heirs, believed they embodied the true will of the French Nation.)

Once power is secured, the elite identifies itself with the state and buttresses its representation of the General Will with the prestige of the state. The state becomes the representative of the General Will; that Will always is what it ought to be; and what it ought to be is determined by the ideological certainties the revolutionist holds: Liberty, Equality, Fraternity, and the victory of the Revolutionary Nation; or the *Herrschaft* of the German *Volk;* or the dictatorship of the proletariat and the establishment of world Communism.

The Liberal-Collectivist Theory of the State

As with the other revolutionary movements of modern times, the politics of liberal collectivism is a Rousseauian politics. It is only in terms parallel to those which are so starkly clear when we look at these other revolutionary movements that we can bring the elements—bureaucratic elite, state, "people"— which are the basic concepts of the liberal-collectivist theory of the state into a coherent whole. The connecting link, as in these parallel theories, is the General Will with all its ambiguity. But the terms of the ambiguity here are different than in Fascism or Communism; for racial *Volk* and *Führer,* for Proletariat and Party, are substituted "the people" and the bureaucratic elite.

The first of these terms is very close to the first term in Rousseau's original position; the "people" as ultimate authority is a concept very similar to Rousseau's concept of the sovereign social body, whose will is the General Will. As with Rousseau, but differing from the Communists and the Nazis, there is no explicit mention of the second term. The liberal collectivist justifies political and social action as the "will of the people" and decides what the content of that will is in terms of the concepts and interests of the ruling bureaucratic elite. The function of the third term of this politics, the state, is to enforce upon people as they actually are, that is, upon individual persons, their own supposed will, that is, the program of the bureaucracy.

Hallowed by the doctrine, unchallenged in a democratic society, that it represents the will of the people, the state can be utilized to consolidate the power of the bureaucratic elite which controls it. Step by step it can move against all other centers of power towards a unified power structure.

The liberal-collectivist bureaucratic elite has little direct resemblance to the conscious unity of, say, a Communist Party. It is quadripartite, not unified. Its four parts (governmental, corporate–trade union, mass communications, and academic) are often more conscious of their differences and rivalries than of their common aims. But the identity of their underlying ideology impels them to a common front whenever and wherever basic issues are raised that would tend towards the restoration of the conditions of freedom. When they struggle among themselves, it is to gain some particular advantage for one group or another within the general bureaucratic system. Any radical challenge to the basic concepts upon which the power of the state is based, they unite instinctively to oppose with all the resources of their immense power. The state is their hope and their future. Without it their very function would disappear, and they would cease to be bureaucrats engineering their segment of the grand design to reconstruct mankind.

How, in what image, the reconstruction will proceed has become somewhat confused—there are a dozen variations on the image of the future for collectivist liberals, and this diversity of detail is what distinguishes them from conscious totalitarians; but to reconstruct, to shape, to control—this remains the constant, and it is this which seals their similarity to the totalitarian. Where God Himself created individual men free each to choose and shape his own life, the liberal collectivists, like all collectivists, like all Rousseauians, perpetrate a double *hubris:* to take God's place as creator and to know better than God— to know that the enforcement of their design upon the individual man is a higher good for him than he could achieve by exercise of his own free choice.

This view of man and the universe could not have brought us to our present pass without the power of the state to effectuate it. Men of powerful intellect and personality might affect the consciousness of an age by their persuasiveness alone, but without command of state power they could not ride roughshod over the innate resistance of human beings to ideas that violate their essential being. Error may long persist on the basis of the intellectual skill or the charisma of its perpetrators; but without the power the state gives it to destroy opposition, its incongruity with the real nature of man will in the end defeat it. Other errors will come along, for this is integral to the process in which free human beings move towards truth. But no one of them can survive indefinitely in its distortion of reality *unless it controls the centralized power with which to drive truth underground, to prevent it from being heard.* Only one institution with such power is conceivable—the state swollen beyond its natural functions.

LEVIATHAN UNDIMINISHED:
The New Conservatism and the State

There is this much truth to John Stuart Mill's doctrine that truth will always prevail in the free market place of ideas, and this much only: given a society free of the power of a totalizing state, truth will survive alongside all the errors and will outlive each of them. Nor, given the human condition, can we expect more. Freedom, which is of the human essence, implies the possibility of producing error as well as finding truth. To achieve a good society requires men unremittingly devoted to the pursuit of good and truth, but it requires also that no one have the power to impose beliefs by force upon other men— and this whether those beliefs be false or true.

It is clear why this is so if the beliefs are false; it is more

difficult to see why this is still so if they are true. Why cannot
state power, if held by governors imbued with true principle,
be used to force virtue upon men? Why should error not be
forcibly destroyed? The answer lies, as I hope what I have written has demonstrated, in the nature of man and of virtue. The
only "virtue" that can be enforced would be a virtue that consisted in conforming one's behavior to external dictation.
Truly to be able to choose good and truth requires a freedom
which, unfortunately, also makes it possible for men to choose
evil and error. In a word, good and truth cannot be enforced,
because by their essential nature they cannot be made real in
men unless they are freely chosen.

At the political level, therefore (that is, at the level which has
to do with power in the social order), the essential requisite for
a good society is such a division of power that no single center
will be able to enforce beliefs upon men by force, or to inhibit
and destroy other beliefs by force. This principle can be reduced to a simpler maxim: The state must be limited to its
proper function of preserving order. But this will only be possible when the person is considered as the central moral entity
and society as but a set of relations between persons, not as an
organism morally superior to persons. For if society be given a
moral status superior to persons, then it follows both implicitly
and logically that society has the right to create an arm to enforce its moral rights. That arm can only be the unlimited Leviathan state: if ultimate moral righteousness rests in society, it is
justified in enforcing its righteousness, and the state which is
its arm cannot be limited by any rights inherent in individual
persons.

Pitfalls of "Community"

Therefore, resistance to the growing collectivist tyranny of the
century requires a theory of society and of the state that has as
its first principle the vindication of the person. It is at this

point—in its attitude towards the person and society—that the New Conservatism fails most signally to offer resistance to collectivist liberalism.

It is not that the New Conservatives have the urge to plan and engineer the social order; they have no stake, ideological or material, in the hegemony of the bureaucratic elite; their detestation of the values and the goals of collectivist liberalism is strong and certain; their criticism of the effects of liberal collectivism on the life of our time is penetrating and effective. No one has written with more eloquence and feeling of the horrors of a gradually collectivizing society than Russell Kirk or Robert A. Nisbet. Kirk[33] and Nisbet[34] delineate the process of dehumanization of the individual human being today with admirable precision and with deep concern for the oppression of personality in a collectivizing society.

Yet both of them, like the other New Conservatives, are blind to the effective cause of the conditions they describe with such justified loathing. The weight of the collective, of "society," upon the individual person, limiting his access to the transcendental sources of his being, to the foundations of value outside history and outside society: this is the prime cause of the human *malaise* which the New Conservatives describe so well. The "social boredom," the "alienation," which Kirk and Nisbet lament, is not the result of a "loss of community," but the result of an excess of state-enforced community. For "community" (except as it is freely created by free individual persons), community conceived as a principle of social order prior and superior to the individual person, can justify any oppression of individual persons so long as it is carried out in the name of "community," of society or of its agent, the state.

This is the principle of collectivism; and it remains the prin-

33. Kirk, "The Problem of Social Boredom," in *A Program for Conservatives.*
34. Robert A. Nisbet, "The Loss of Community," in *The Quest for Community* (New York: Oxford University Press, 1953).

ciple of collectivism even though the New Conservatives who speak of "community" would prefer a congeries of communities based upon locality, occupation, belief, caste, class, traditional ties, to the totalizing and equalizing national or international community which is the goal of the collectivists. This is to their credit. Better a multitude of enforced collectivities, so that the individual human being may wrest for himself an area of autonomy out of simultaneous partial loyalty to several of them or out of precarious existence in the interstices between them, than a single all-embracing Leviathan community which will totally subordinate him. But what the New Conservatives will not see is that there are no solid grounds on which the kind of "community" they propose as the end towards which social existence should be ordered can be defended against the kind of "community" the collectivists propose.

Their defense may be based on taste, on preference for one kind of superindividual organism rather than another; but then there is no fundamental reason why their position should prevail over that of the collectivist. Or they could claim that the network of multitudinous "communities" which they prefer is less of a threat to the freedom of the individual person. But this argument in favor of their kind of community over the collectivists' depends upon a primary judgment that individual persons are the entities in terms of which the goodness or badness of the social order should be judged. This defense, however, the New Conservatives reject. Putting the individual person at the center of political thought is to them the greatest of political and social evils. Caught within the pattern of concepts inherited from classical political theory, they cannot free themselves from the doctrine that men find their true being only as organic parts of a social entity, from which and in terms of which their lives take value. Hence the New Conservatives cannot effectively combat the essential political error of collectivist liberalism: its elevation of corporate society and the state which stands as the enforcing agency of corporate society to the level of final political ends.

Apotheosis of the State

The evils around us they see, but the underlying causes of those evils they cannot understand. Russell Kirk, for example, using so apparently innocent an example as the federal government's school lunch program, can show how the liberal-collectivist bureaucracy—putatively executing "the will of the people" and on the most seemingly benevolent of motives—penetrates into hitherto local and private concerns of individual citizens. But in the next breath he will castigate the central axiom upon which a political theory that could resist such usurpations must be based.

Critical though he is of the growth of centralized state power, he insists, following Burke, that "society is an immortal being . . . a *spiritual* entity."[35] And, as always when the set of interrelations between individual human beings that is social existence is raised to the level of a being endowed with corporate personality, the one error is followed logically and inevitably by another and even more dangerous one. The apotheosis of society leads directly to a theoretical concept of the state which would foreclose effective opposition to the totalizing state of contemporary society. Once it is believed that society is a being, society has rights. And by the very magnitude of its stature as compared with that of any individual person, those rights overshadow and take unlimited precedence over the rights of individual persons. A being of such grandeur that it is a veritable god, containing and expressing terrestrial existence, must have the right and the power to defend itself and to execute its will. From the deification of society arises the

35. Kirk, *The Conservative Mind*, 18, emphasis in original.

deification of the state, which is society in its active aspect. Believing that "society is a spiritual entity," it becomes impossible for the New Conservatives to see the state as physical power in the hands of a specific group of human beings. It becomes impossible to understand that the state, though a necessity of human existence, has an unlimited potential for evil the moment its power increases beyond the strict necessities of its function.

These disciples of Edmund Burke, however, believe with him that the state is a divine organ without whose positive action men cannot achieve virtue, that "He Who gave our nature to be perfected by our virtue, willed also the necessary means of its perfection.—He willed therefore the state—He willed its connexion with the source and original archetype of all perfection."[36]

So Russell Kirk:

> Government is . . . a device of Divine wisdom to supply human wants. . . . The government may justly perform all those labors which surpass the reach of individual abilities. . . . [37]

It is true Mr. Kirk includes among the desirable ends of state activity "to secure every man in his natural liberty," and this is excellent. But he adds "and to advance the culture of society," thus, by proposing for the state unnatural and swollen power, negating the end of liberty. Throughout his writing he makes it clear that, though he dislikes many of the activities of the contemporary state, he will not accept in principle its limitation to its essential functions. Insisting with Burke that society has a divine being and that from it the state derives a mystique independent of its limited function as an instrument of persons, he polemicizes against any political theory based upon the primacy of the individual person.

No doubt a state controlled by men imbued with Mr. Kirk's

36. Burke, *Works*, vol. 2, 370.
37. Kirk, *Beyond the Dreams of Avarice*, 146–47.

principles would enforce and encourage social and cultural conditions highly superior to those enforced and encouraged by contemporary collectivism, whether welfarist, socialist, or Communist. Such men might even voluntarily limit the use of the power available to them through the state—though this is questionable, considering the tendency of power to corrupt and the historical record of the best of men when in command of power. But what is important on the level of political theory is not what uses men wish to make of power, but whether power theoretically unlimited (as it is bound to be if society and the state are considered as beings superior to individual persons) can possibly conduce to a good social order.

The Enforcement of Virtue, a Persistent Delusion

What the New Conservatives are saying is that the state is the proper organ for the enforcement of virtue. When this concept is combined with the antecedent concept of society as a primary moral being, the individual person's control over his destiny, his freedom to search for and to choose virtue, is absorbed into the destiny of society. Its virtue must be his virtue—which is no more nor less than the central tenet of totalitarianism.

Walter Berns, who (though he refuses to call himself a New Conservative) expresses these concepts with great ability and force, insists that "government should seek to . . . promote the virtue of citizens"[38] and calls upon the classical tradition of political theory to support his argument that virtue, not freedom, is the primary principle of the state. Once again the conditions of classical society, of the society of the *polis,* are taken as the norm of human existence. The basic philosophical position of the great classical political theorists, which reflected the limitations of their vision, is elevated as the prime law of moral-

38. Walter Berns, *Freedom, Virtue and the First Amendment* (Baton Rouge: Louisiana State University Press, 1957), 256.

political existence; their highest insights, which broke through those limitations and glimpsed the concept of the person as the center of moral existence, are forgotten. The Aristotle who wrote " . . . in order to be good one must be in a certain state when one does the several acts, i.e., one must do them as a result of choice and for the sake of the acts themselves"[39] is forgotten, while the Aristotle who expressed the fundamental Greek outlook, that man is primarily not an autonomous person but a *polis* animal, is taken as an oracle.

Certainly the concern of the New Conservatives with the achievement of virtue is a just concern. Ultimately this is the most important of problems. All that I am contending is that it is not a *political* problem, that it is not the concern of the state, that virtue cannot be enforced or brought about by political means. Political thought and political action must be concerned with establishing and maintaining the conditions of freedom. True, freedom, though it is the end of political theory and political action, is not the end of men's existence. It is a condition, a decisive and integral condition, but still only a *condition* of that end, which is virtue. The New Conservatives are right when they insist that a consideration of men in society must come to grips with the problem of virtue. They are only wrong in demanding that that problem be solved by the exercise of political power. But here their error is a serious one, for it is an error which they share with the collectivists who care not at all for virtue or for freedom.

By their insistence on the use of political power for the inculcation of virtue, by their refusal to take a principled position in defense of a state limited to establishing the conditions of freedom, they disqualify themselves as effective opponents of liberal collectivism. The New Conservatives are left neither the champions of Leviathan that the collectivist liberals are nor the enemies of Leviathan that the principled conservatives are, but mere critical observers of Leviathan undiminished.

39. Aristotle *Nicomachean Ethics* 6.12.1144a.

6

THE LOCUS OF VIRTUE

The question may justly be asked: if the function of the state is to be limited to the establishment and protection of a free order, if the enforcement or the inculcation of virtue is beyond its rightful power, where in the social order is the authority that will guide men in virtuous paths? Before directly answering that question, it is necessary to consider some of the answers often given, answers which attempt to substitute other collective institutions for the state as enforcers of virtue. Collectivist liberalism, of course, has no answer because it cannot conceive of limitations upon the power of the state. After all, the democratic state is "we," and what "we" want is by definition virtuous—or (another variation) the just state is ruled by experts and what they decide is right. More fundamentally, however, and more honestly, most of its theoreticians would answer on a philosophical level, in their relativist and positivist mode, that the very concept of virtue is meaningless.

Enforced Community

The proponents of the New Conservatism, to the degree that they are willing to accept limitations upon the power of the state in relation to virtue, fall back upon the concept of "community," and look to it as the source of moral authority in the social order. They see the danger of the aggrandizing modern state; but, although they fear its drive towards totalitarianism, they react with equal vigor against the idea of a political order grounded in the freedom of individual persons. They are arrayed as fiercely against "individualism" as they are against totalitarianism.

Russell Kirk is eloquent on this subject, to the point of denying that a man can be at once a Christian and an individualist. Robert A. Nisbet in *The Quest for Community* doggedly maintains that "individualism" and the breakdown of socially enforced community lead directly to totalitarianism. They both see Bentham, Mill, and Spencer as but preparing the way for Marx, Lenin, and Stalin. The line of their argument is this: When men are not held together in customary communities (and "customary" in their usage means "socially enforced") they become "atomized," "alienated,"[40] incapable of resisting the aggrandizement of political power.

Community as here understood is not the voluntary association of individual human beings in the myriad of relationships that are available for each person to choose or to reject in a free society. Nor, in their concept of community as binding, are they limiting themselves to the necessary and inescapable associations that the conditions of existence prescribe for all men: the family, within which everyone is born and raised,[41] and the state without which civilized life is impossible. (I should remind my readers that, however much I have insisted upon the

40. It is interesting how often this word "alienation" turns up in New Conservative writings (as it does also in the writing of "liberal" sociologists and psychologists of the stripe of Erich Fromm) when one remembers the origin of the word as used in this sense. It is the young Karl Marx's concept at the beginning of his theoretical activity; what he presented was the drama of the separation of individual persons from a social matrix by the development of capitalism and the free society of the nineteenth century. His "cure" for the freedom of the individual from state and society and community, the freedom he condemns as "alienation," was . . . socialism.

41. That is, outside the constructions of Plato at his most aridly abstract, or the living nightmare of such Communist realities as the Chinese communes.

great potentiality of the state for evil if it goes beyond its natural bounds, nevertheless I have insisted that, limited to its natural functions, it is necessary for the proper life of men as men.) They mean, and they mean to mean, that the individual person is not the essential end of civil society. Nisbet, disturbed by the dangers of totalitarianism, champions a pluralism—but a pluralism of communities, not a pluralism of persons.

Persons as such are anathema to the New Conservative doctrine, unless they are mere symbols for orders and ranks and hierarchies, stiffly disposed as in a Byzantine mosaic, signifying the abstract virtue of diversity. But Heaven forfend that they be actually diverse, individual human beings, unranked and uncontrolled. There is no place in the New Conservative conspectus for the person as such, for those who live as individuals—"humble to God, haughty to man"—scorning the bounds of a predetermined estate, vindicating the glory of the person as person.

State or Community: False Dilemma

The New Conservatives present us with a false antithesis: either the all-powerful totalitarian state, grinding impersonally and brutally upon the freedom of everyone, or the subtler, quieter tyranny of "customarily" imposed community, in which no one can escape from the deadly environment of hereditarily or geographically imposed association. This antithesis is not only vicious in concept, but false in fact. It is vicious because it is directed to enlisting our repugnance to modern statism in behalf of a gentler tyranny. It is false because—difficult though the human condition is—we are not in actuality faced with the harsh dilemma of choosing between a fiercer and a milder tyranny over the human spirit.

This dilemma is not natural to the human condition; less is it derived from the central tradition of Western civilization; and still less, from the tradition of the American republic. Those who present us with it split asunder the unity in tension by which the West has been able to preserve both the freedom of the person and the authority of truth and good, both freedom in the social order and virtue in the being of men, both the searching spirit and the authority of tradition. We are not faced with the alternative: On the one hand, a social order without values, without standards of truth and beauty and good; a philosophy unfounded on a transcendental end and an ultimate purpose; an ethos at the mercy of vulgarity and power. Or, on the other hand, a social order, Burkean in mode, constrained and controlled by the tyranny of habit, custom, and prescription; a philosophy so held to precedent that it is deprived of the freedom to deepen and develop human understanding; an ethos tightly swaddled in the multitudinous wrappings of code and custom.

These, however, are the alternatives presented to us both explicitly and rhetorically by the champions of "community." Baker Brownell writes: "I doubt whether men can evaluate experience at all, or claim it, except within the integral relevance and context of the community."[42] Or, Martin Buber: "He alone is true to the one Present Being who knows he is bound to his place. . . ."[43] These concepts of the high priests of community subordinate the individual person, made secondary and derivative in value, to a whole of which he becomes but a cellular part. Although this general outlook, which permeates the writings of the New Conservatives, is more elevated in its moral ends than the materialistic subordination of man to the totalizing state that marks the social theory of the collectivist liberals (and all collectivists), it still is characterized by subordination of the person to collective entities.

No, the dilemma is a false construction. There is a third way. The history of the West has been the history of that third way, a

---

42. Baker Brownell, *The Human Community* (New York: Harper & Bros., 1950), 266.

43. Martin Buber, *Between Man and Man* (Boston: Beacon Press, 1955), 70.

way which has held in shimmering tension the authority of truth and the freedom of men. It has done so (sometimes less perfectly, sometimes more perfectly) by recognizing the absolute authority of truth in the intellectual and spiritual realm, while at the same time remaining aware of the contingency of institutions in the social realm and their consequent subordination to the transcendent value of the human person. It has distinguished—in turmoil and strife, it is true, but in the end it has always distinguished—between the fundamental truths that constitute the structure of man's being as a creature with a supernatural destiny, living in the natural world, and man-made certitudes, where authority can only be tyranny because truth is uncertain. Understanding this, the West has always recognized, in the representative moments of its drive towards the incarnation of its vision, that the ultimate guardians of its essential truths could not be the possessors of material authority with their power to impose their own particular version of the truth and with their susceptibility to the corruptions of power. The guardians of intellectual and moral truth, to whom the West has always given its final deference (to the destruction of those who would impose an armored truth) have been the learned, the priestly, the prophetic, skilled in the tradition—men devoted to the priority of persons over institutions, devoted not to power, but to truth and good.

Total state and "plurality of communities" do not constitute an antithesis; rather they are variants—the one, it is true, far more devastating than the other—of the same denial of the primary value, on this earth, of the individual person. The social order in tension between the authority of truth and good and the recognition of the fundamental value of the individual person—this is our heritage. It is the answer to the false antithesis of total state or all-encompassing community: a society armed against positivist nihilism and political messianism on the intellectual and moral level, and against tyranny, open or covert, on the social level.

Person, Association, Institution

If I inveigh against the concept of community as a decisive concept in political and social thought, or insist upon the priority of the individual person to collective groups of any sort, I am not therefore proposing a Robinson Crusoe social theory or maintaining that the person is a monadlike atom, cut off and isolated from other persons. These are the usual accusations brought by the proponents of community against the defenders of freedom. Again they propound a dilemma: Either accept the priority of community to the person or stand convicted of rejecting love, friendship, all mutual action and communion among human beings. But this time, too, the dilemma is unreal; indeed, in this case it turns upon its framers. Only the independence and autonomy of the person makes love or any other valid relationship between persons possible; were human beings but parts of a larger whole, their love, all their reachings out one to another, would be but the cellular interactions dictated by the tropisms of the larger organism.

But we know from every ounce of our experience that this is not so. When we love, when we think or act mutually, when we create associations or institutions, each of us knows that this is *his* act, *his* reaching out voluntarily, to establish concert with other human beings; when we worship, each of us knows that it is *his* reaching out to the Person that is God. The dilemma is false: only individual persons, conscious each in his own uniqueness, can reach out and establish relations with other persons, relations charged with the content, vibrant with the tone, that all of us know unmistakably on the basis of our direct awareness. To assert the freedom and independence of the individual person implies no denial of the value of mutuality, of association and common action between persons. It only denies the value of coerced association.

When men are free, they will of course form among themselves a multitude of associations to fulfill common purposes when common purposes exist. The potential relationships between one man and other men are multifarious; but they are relationships between independent, conscious, self-acting beings. They are not the interactions of cells of a larger organism. When they are voluntary, freely chosen to fulfill the mutual needs of independent beings, they are fruitful and indeed essential. But they are essential only in that *some* kind of relationship to other men is essential to the nature of man. They are, as it were, essential as a *genus*—a general class of thing that human beings need; no specific imposed association as such is essential. Each man will find, as a free being, the relationships congenial to his specific needs.

The Family

To this completely voluntary character of associations proper to the free nature of men, there are only two exceptions—the state and the family. Neither can be voluntary because of the human condition itself. The reasons why the one, the state, is essential (however dangerous its improper aggrandizement may be) I have discussed. But it is, as I have tried to prove, irrelevant to the question posed in this chapter—the locus of the guidance of men towards virtue—because its proper concern is not the inculcation of virtue but the preservation of an order conducive to freedom. The family is the condition into which children are born and under which they develop as human beings. As far as they are concerned, it is not voluntary—but (*pace* the worship of the child that has sprung up in the twentieth-century world) neither are children as yet persons in the full sense of the word; in any social order where firm values are respected, they are potential persons, being moulded into true persons by the imposition upon them of the values of their tradition and their culture. As far as their parents are concerned, the family is, however, entered into voluntarily;

marriage is, in a free society, originally a mutual voluntary act of two individuals—voluntary, even though any marriage worthy of that exalted name is an unbreakable compact and though the family, proceeding from marriage, creates morally indissoluble bonds of parental obligation.

The family is the most important form through which virtue is inculcated in children. But it is not the institution of the family as such that inculcates virtue; it is the persons who constitute the family—father and mother and other close relatives—who in actuality decide the issue of the moral and intellectual direction that children take. And this is so even if, as has become the mode today, an increasing majority of parents shrug their shoulders of this responsibility and turn their children over to the state and other institutions for 90 percent of their waking hours—to schools and a myriad of groupist organizations from Cub Scouts to Little Leagues, and to the great moral teachers of the television fraternity. By following this mode, parents, as responsible persons, deliberately act in a contravirtuous way. It is not institutions, but their own personal conscious choice that destroys the conditions of virtue for their children. The family as an institution cannot guarantee the raising of the young in the paths of virtue, although the family is a necessary form; only individual persons, acting through the form of the family, can do so.

So it is with the other institutions and associations into which men enter. It is not some mystical quality of "community" which makes these institutions and associations conducive to the growth of virtue. They will assist or impede that great human endeavor, depending upon their form; but the positive content of the endeavor will always arise from the beliefs, the understanding, the devotion of the individual persons who associate themselves. The form of institutions has no power to make bad men good or good men bad. They can, under circumstances of the kind we have seen too much of in this unhappy century, restrict freedom and undermine the respon-

sibility of the individual so that they become a serious impedi-
ment to the growth of virtue; but they cannot, of their own
power, make men good. At their best, they can create favorable
conditions—and that is all.

The Economic Order

Thus, a prevailing mystique of our era is the belief that a transformation of the economic relations into which men enter
can, somehow, magically solve human problems and create virtue. The modern source of this belief is Marxism, with its
quasi-religious dogmatic certainty that direction of the economy by the state will bring about a paradise on earth. But it is
not in the Marxist form that this general idea has effectively
penetrated our society; our collectivist liberals, shunning the
sharp dogmatic mode of the Marxists, have adopted a more
pragmatic approach to salvation by economic reconstruction—
the prescriptions of John Maynard Keynes and the more sophisticated contemporary variants of his doctrines.

The New Conservatives are not, like the collectivist liberals,
missionaries for the Keynesian system, but they fail utterly to
see its dangers and they concentrate their attacks in the economic sphere upon the principled proponents of a free capitalist economy as "Benthamite individualists." They miss—as,
considering their radical devaluation of freedom, they are
bound to miss—the decisive virtue of a free economy: the re-
striction of the power of the state. Much else could be urged in
its defense: it gives to the individual person, the consumer,
rather than to the bureaucratic planner with state power the
decision as to what should be and what should not be produced; it has been under its aegis that the enormous growth of
human productivity in modern times has occurred. But these
virtues are secondary to the preservation of the conditions of
freedom by holding from the state the control of a large segment of human life.

Some of the champions of the free economy, it is true, tend
to fall into the same error as their collectivist opponents and to
maintain that a free economy is itself a guarantee of a good
and virtuous life. To the degree that this claim is put forward,
the New Conservative criticism is just. A free economy can no
more bring about virtue than a state-controlled economy. A
free economy is, however, necessary in the modern world for
the preservation of freedom, which is the condition of a virtuous society.

The issue is not, as it is often posed, whether Keynesian economics will "work." Many economic systems "work"—granted
the ends towards which they are directed. Tribal economy
worked. Oriental despotism worked. Capitalism works, socialism works, Communism works. But the truly important question is not whether an economic system "works," but, working,
what ends it subserves. If this criterion is held in view and the
determination of human existence by material forces is rejected, economics must be subordinated to moral and political
philosophy. The issue becomes not merely that a given economic system work, but that it be conducive to proper ends. To
say that economics is a subordinate discipline does not mean
that in its own sphere it should be censored in its methods of
enquiry or in the objectivity of its conclusions. Economics is
closest to an exact science of all the disciplines that study men
and society. It is at the same time the farthest removed from
philosophical competence, from the capacity to establish value.
Economics can neither establish nor confute the validity of a
moral system or a political system. What it can do is to demonstrate what the results of alternate courses of economic action
will be. The choice between these sets of results (and therefore
between the economic systems which lead to them) is beyond
the prerogative of economics. It is a moral and political choice.

For the defense of freedom, the decisive criterion of any economic system today is whether it gives to the state or withholds
from it control of the economy. Keynesism is an alternative to
Marxism as a mode of state control of the economy; and while

its methods are slower than the methods of Marxism, more indirect in their application, it has proved far more successful
than Marxism in aggrandizing the power of the state in countries with advanced economies. Only in industrially backward
countries—or where, for example, as in Czechoslovakia, Communist physical force has prevailed—has the road to statism
been the Marxist road of nationalization of the means of production. So successful has the Keynesian movement towards
state control of the economy proven to be in industrially advanced countries (under the slogans of "progressive capitalism" or "the mixed economy"), that the very Socialist parties
of such countries have given up their Marxism to embrace the
more effective Keynesian methods. The most significant of
these methods are (1) state control of credit and of the interest
rate, either directly or through a state-dominated central bank-
ing system; (2) "a somewhat comprehensive socialization of
investment";[44] (3) "measures for the re-distribution of
income,"[45] primarily through punitive taxation and state-
induced inflation; (4) "the euthanasia of the rentier [that is,
the "painless" doing away with those who have acquired capital, either through their own efforts or through inheritance]
and, consequently, the euthanasia of the cumulative oppressive
power of the capitalist to exploit the scarcity-value of capital"[46]—which, since the scarcity-value of capital cannot itself be
eliminated, means that the usufructs of capital will be gradually transferred to the state.

Keynesism justifies—nay demands—an open and uncon-
cealed use of the powers of the state to secure for the state a
directing control over the economy; and its techniques, originally popularized as cures for depression, can be as readily em-
ployed to increase statist and bureaucratic power in prosperous

44. John Maynard Keynes, *The General Theory of Employment, Interest, and
Money* (New York: Harcourt, Brace & Co., 1936), 378.
45. Ibid., 373.
46. Ibid., 376.

times. John Kenneth Galbraith condescends to Keynes as old-fashioned, but the measures he proposes, to bring a still larger share of the national income under the control of the state, are the same measures of fiscal manipulation and punitive taxation that the influence of Keynes institutionalized in the "mixed economy." Where Keynes thought that the capitalists did not know how to invest and that bureaucrats could do it better by state manipulation, Galbraith thinks that consumers do not know how to spend and that bureaucrats can do it better for them by transferring purchasing power from "the private sector" to "the public sector," that is, from individual persons to the state.

The doctrines of Lord Keynes, and of the heirs of Lord Keynes, lead directly to the siphoning off of a large proportion of the property of individual persons into the hands of the state. By that token, the power of the state is swollen, and the power of persons to stand firmly on their own, independent of the state and of the pressure of any collective influence, is progressively weakened; free citizens steadily deteriorate into wards of the state. The Keynesian system leads insensibly to "euthanasia" of the free energy of persons—in its end it parallels the Marxist system, different though its methods are. The welfare state—that is, the state that draws into itself function after function that belongs to individual men (provision for the eventualities of sickness, unemployment, accident, variations in market conditions; the education of children; responsibility for the care of aging members of the family: all the vicissitudes of life) is founded upon Keynesian and neo-Keynesian doctrines. The ends towards which it moves are the security of the anthill or the beehive and the transformation of free men into a state-enforced similitude to the ants and the bees, creatures whose existence is social tropism.

The economic order dictated by Keynesian concepts, in this respect like the economic order dictated by Marxist concepts, is flatly evil because it moves towards the destruction of personal freedom. The free capitalist economic order does not in itself and cannot in itself move towards virtue. It does not and cannot directly inculcate virtue; but it does, by foreclosing state control of the economy and guaranteeing the possibility of individual economic independence to some and free economic choice to all in an economy of high productivity, conduce to freedom for the person. Like all established sets of relationships between human beings, like all associations and institutions, an economic system cannot of itself be a source of virtue; it can only either inhibit the possibility of virtue by suppressing the freedom of men or indirectly conduce to virtue by helping to make men free.

The Educational System

The economic order is, in the scale of human relationships, at something of a remove from the direct problem of the inculcation of virtue. The same principles, however, apply at every level of the relationships between men and of the associational and institutional manifestations of those relationships. Consider the relationships into which men enter to provide for the education of the young—an area more directly related to the inculcation of virtue.

The symptoms of deterioration in our educational system, long apparent to serious observers, have become so obvious that the fact of deterioration is now a matter of public concern. Everyone except the educational bureaucrats, whose vested interests are at stake, and those collectivist liberals to whom any attack on any state institution is impermissible (for our educational system has become in its decisive sector an arm of the state) agrees that something has gone wrong. But what? Why is it that the massive contemporary expenditure of time and energy and interest on education accumulates so little learning in the mind of the student? Why does he acquire so degraded a sense of values, so little direction towards virtue? Starkly, in the corruption of our children, we stand face to face with the truth that it is men and the ideas they hold that decide all the most important questions; that, as Richard Weaver has so eloquently shown, "ideas have consequences" and that it is the men who are imbued with these ideas—not the institutional forms through which they operate—who bring about these consequences.

The present state of American education is the direct consequence of the instrumentalist philosophy of John Dewey. Applied to the educational process and transmitted to the American educational system through an institutional network of associations, training schools, and publications, instrumentalist theories have, in two generations, annihilated the education that, in one form or another, has for a thousand years formed the men who made Western civilization. This education, inherited from Hellenic civilization and transmuted by Christianity, moulded the men who developed Western civilization—moulded the framers of our Constitution, the founders of the Republic. It was based on the assumption that the function of the school and the college is to train the mind and transmit to the young the culture and tradition of the civilization, thus forming a firm foundation for virtue.

This assumption implied the acceptance of certain other assumptions of a philosophical kind: that there is such a thing as truth; that the tradition of Western civilization embodies the highest truths that, by the aid of reason and grace, men have been able to attain; that the criterion of value on this earth is innately the individual person, so that the claims of "society," "community," and state are secondary to and derived from him. It implied, also, definite social and political beliefs: that, although all men are created with certain inalienable rights, individuals vary in capacity and ability; that, therefore, to deprive the able of the opportunity to realize their ability, in the name of a leveling equalitarianism, is as great an oppression as to enslave the many for the benefit of the few. And it involved an important psychological presupposition: that education can be acquired only at the cost of work and pain.

The prescriptions which today define the practice of our educational system leave scarcely a trace of the great concepts of Western education. It is not that the training of the mind and the transmission of the truths asserted by our civilization have been forgotten; they have been deliberately and consciously eliminated. Those who have done the eliminating have made no secret of their intentions; they have branded these concepts as reactionary and obscurantist. For the instrumentalist there can be no value tradition worth transmitting; virtue as an end of human existence is a superstition left over from the Middle Ages; what is right and good and true is what serves as an instrument for adjustment to the society around one. The aim of education must be "life adjustment," and the method "life experience." The teacher must "impose" nothing. His role is not to teach the wisdom that a great civilization and a great nation have made available, but to "cooperate" with the child in gaining "acquaintance with the changing world," where "experience" and "free activity" will somehow, magically, educate him. Thus, he will grow up free of the "stifling authoritarianism" of the old education and become independent of mind and will.

But it is nonsense to assume that because the young are not firmly taught in the ways of virtue and drilled into serious habits of thought, they will spontaneously develop an educated independence of belief and thought. What will happen instead is what is happening. The teacher, free from the responsibility of teaching "abstract values" in a disciplined manner, has to fill the gap with something. Under pressure to bring about "adjustment" to the environment, he fills it with the current prejudices of his environment—and the prejudices of a contemporary educationist or a teacher trained by educationists are certain to reflect the prevailing value nihilism and political collectivism.

Furthermore, under the presuppositions upon which contemporary education functions, the very ability to think is destroyed. To learn to think requires effort and pain. There being no pressure to exert effort or to undergo pain, the mental habits of run-of-the-mill students become simply slovenly, while the tendency is for the bright ones to develop into brash youngsters in whom flashes of brilliance only emphasize the lack of intellectual depth. True, there are exceptions—hard-thinking young people, whose salvation from the smothering norm is the result of the surviving vestiges of firm and principled home influence, the providential and increasing presence of a few good teachers in our educational institutions, and, in recent years, the growing revolt among students against the whole structure of collectivist liberalism.

The decline of the American educational system to its present state is a classical demonstration of the thesis I have been affirming: that the inculcation of virtue depends not upon the institutional relations among men, but upon individual persons and the ideas they hold; and that institutions at their best can only create favorable conditions for individual men to act rightly, while, when they attain a collectivist authority, they inhibit the action of individual men for the good. The state of our educational system today is directly the result of the actions of men who have been imbued with fallacious ideas, and they alone are directly responsible. They were much facilitated in gaining decisive influence, however, by an institutional revolution that transformed the relation of education to the state. The preconditions for the triumph of Deweyism in education and the consequent decay of education were created by a process which set in more than a hundred years ago, long before the period of John Dewey's influence. The invasion of the field of education by tax-supported state authority—itself based on ideas of a statist nature—was the first great breach in the concept of government limited in power to the maintenance of internal and external order, the concept upon which the Republic was founded. The movement for universal, "free" (i.e., tax-supported), compulsory education begins simultaneously with the emergence in American history, in the person of Andrew Jackson, of the type Franklin D. Roosevelt brought to perfection, the demagogic "leader of the people." By the turn of the century the movement was largely successful. The decay of the quality of American education had already alarmed many eminent observers, and the foundation had been laid for the debacle of the past thirty years.

The principle that all men are equal before the law, which is essential to the moral functioning of a limited state, becomes steadily and disastrously distorted when the state engages in activities beyond its natural functions. Equality before the law—a principle based upon the innate and incommensurable value of each individual created person—is transformed into a universal equalitarianism that ludicrously insists upon the equality of all persons in all respects. Therefore, once the state steps in, the equal ability and potentiality of everyone must be assumed. All must be educated "equally" and in the same way. When, further, as a result of the intervention of the state, education falls under the control of a bureaucracy that acts upon these premises, the very idea of quality in education inevitably goes by the board. The end becomes not the development of the spirit of man, but its acclimatization to the mediocrity of the mass mind. It took a long time for these potentialities of state-controlled education to unfold, for the effect of the institutional environment to be fully felt, for good men and true ideas to be effectively inhibited. But the institutional situation was by its nature destructive of those who stood for quality and virtue, and favorable to their opposites. When John Dewey and his followers came along, the road was open. With quality, virtue, and differentiation ruled out, their ideas gained an easy ascendancy.

When these considerations are adduced, the answer usually is this: Be that as it may, without state intervention education of any kind would have been severely restricted to the few. So uncritically is this belief held that it is never argued, only assumed. Yet, can there be any doubt that if the state had not intervened, there would have been as multifarious, diverse, and brilliant a growth of educational opportunities through the enterprise of private individuals and independent groups as has taken place in other fields? Given the free action of individuals and groups—fired by beliefs and concepts as to what education should be and moved by the spirit of charity or motivated by the hope of profit—if the false theories of Deweyism had gained influence in some institutions of a competitive educational network, its obvious inferiority would soon have put them out of business. Or, at the least, that inferiority would have restricted their patronage to those who could not recognize superiority. Competition would have made educational opportunities as common as it has made the automobile.

The entrance of the state into education, moving inevitably through quasi monopoly towards monopoly, crushes all differentiation. Its opening of the way to leveling theories, dedicated to assuring that no unworthy son of a wealthy father shall receive an education he does not deserve, has made it certain that no one, rich or poor, can receive an education pitched above the mediocre. When the mediocre becomes the standard, as it inevitably does if differentiation is ruled out and education is judged by the degree to which it can adapt to the average, not only is quality destroyed, but with it is destroyed the very possibility of an education capable of laying the foundations for a virtuous life. For virtue does not become the end of a person's existence by "other directed" adjustment to the norm or through the apotheosis of the "experience" of the natural, untaught, doctrineless young. Standards of virtue are the hard-won prize of millennia of civilization, and they can only be inculcated in the young by men devoted to them and skilled in their understanding of them—men who will teach with authority the traditions of the civilization and the doctrines of virtue. Teachers imbued with Deweyan and similar ideas are obviously incapable of fulfilling this responsibility; they are, in fact, hostile to the very thought of its fulfillment.

The present failure of American education to perform its function is the failure of individual persons to perform their functions. The institutional characteristics of the educational system do indeed make the advancement of the wrong kind of teacher and the suppression of the right kind easier, but as an institution it does and can do no worse than that. If it were properly established, it could do no better than encourage the advancement of teachers dedicated to the inculcation of virtue and discourage their opposites. Everything depends upon the individual persons who do the teaching and upon the beliefs and ideas they hold. The locus of virtue in the education of the young lies in the persons who teach them. In the schools and colleges, as throughout the social order, it is individual persons who are decisive.

The Locus of Virtue in the Social Order: The Individual Person

The priority of the person and the derivative character of suprapersonal entities, analyzed in this discussion of the economic system and the educational system, apply with equal force to all sets of relationships between men. Those relationships may be of the kind best described as institutions, or as associations, or as communities. They may be in their essential form necessary to human existence, like the state and the family. They may fulfill a function which is necessary, but which can be fulfilled in many different ways, like the economic system or the educational system. Or they may be totally voluntary, like a professional association, or a charitable guild, or a chess club. But all of them are instrumentalities only. Depending upon their structure, they can make the movement of human beings towards virtue easier or more difficult—but that is all.[47] The institution, the association, the community, is neither virtuous nor unvirtuous, and cannot itself inculcate virtue. Only individual persons can do this.

Individual persons cannot, of course, be virtuous or guide others to virtue by their own unaided powers. There is a moral and intellectual order, based upon the constitution of being, grasped and interpreted by generation upon generation, upon which men must draw. But the knowledge, the understanding, the belief, which that intellectual and moral order represents, has meaning only for sentient human beings, not for any suprahuman collectivity—institution, association, or community. Truth has meaning only for persons; beauty illumines the consciousness only of persons; virtue can be pursued only by persons.

A social order is a good social order to the degree that men live as free persons under conditions in which virtue can be

47. It is advisedly that I have omitted from this discussion what is the most important of the associations related to the inculcation of virtue: the association for the worship of God, the church. Questions are involved here that go much deeper than the political or the social; and I am not personally able, at this point in my life, to speak with certainty on these questions.

That no civilization can come into being or develop without being informed by one kind or another of relationship between the men who make it up and God, I am certain; that Christianity, which informs Western civilization, is the highest and deepest relationship to the Divine that men can attain, I am also certain; but I am not able to say that any single institutional church is the bearer of God's spirit on earth. And this makes it impossible for me to discuss the church in the terms of this book. At the very least, it is of the category of those institutions which fulfill a function that is necessary, but which can be fulfilled in a number of different ways. If, however, it should be true that a single church is the direct expression of God's love for men, then that church would be, like the state and the family, necessary in its essential form to human existence.

In either case, the association of human beings for the worship of God, the church, is, of all human associations, the most important and the most directly related to the inculcation of virtue. But still it is individual persons in that association who, with the sustenance of God's grace, themselves as persons are virtuous or not, inculcate virtue or fail to do so.

freely realized, advanced, and perpetuated. Freedom has its risks because it may not be virtue but vice that men advance, but all existence has its risks. Unless men are free to be vicious, they cannot be virtuous. No community can make them virtuous. Nor can any community force upon them conditions antagonistic to virtue if the state does not, with its power, give coercive strength to community and so long as the state, fulfilling its limited but necessary functions, protects individual persons from force and fraud by other persons and associations of persons.

The person is the locus of virtue. No other men, no associations of other men, can deprive him of the freedom to pursue virtue and inculcate virtue in others, if the state is maintained in its limited function, giving no sanction to the imposition of coercion by men upon men and protecting each man from coercion by his fellows.

CONCLUSION

THE SHACKLING
OF LEVIATHAN

Belief in the primacy of the person was inherent from the beginning in the vision which formed Western civilization. The complementary concept of freedom as the determining criterion of the good political and social order was, however, only partially realized, either theoretically or practically, until the foundation of the American republic and the framing of our Constitution. Here for the first time a polity was established based upon the freedom of the person as its end and upon firm limitation of the powers of the state as the means to achieve that end.

For half a century or more the idea was clearly and firmly held, and the practice of the American republic closely approximated the idea. But a process of retrogression set in, first slowly, then faster and faster—a process in which the decisive moments were the introduction of mass democratism by Andrew Jackson, undermining of the sovereignty of the several states by Abraham Lincoln, and the naturalization in the United States of twentieth-century collectivist principles and methods by Franklin D. Roosevelt. During the past thirty years that process has been frighteningly accelerated. A polity which represented the drive of men towards the full potentialities of their being has been defiled; that drive, more magnificent than any drive in the physical universe towards the moon, the planets, or beyond, has been slowed down, cut short, reversed.

That there should set in a retreat from the vision of a truly free social order, and from the difficult and demanding endeavor to realize a polity that makes such an order possible, was perhaps to be expected. Before the advent of the Western concept of the person, men had lived for thousands of years of civilization and tens of thousands of years of precivilized human existence under conditions in which freedom was only an occasional and barely grasped concept, only a fugitive reality. But, however harsh the pressures of life, they lived in the deep security of the enveloping social womb. Freedom brings men rudely and directly face to face with their own personal responsibility for their own free actions. This is a shock. Remembrance of the fleshpots of enveloping security ever tugs insidiously at the souls of free men. But where mind and will have been clear and firm, the temptation has been rejected.

It is confusion of mind and consequent debilitation of will that have brought the United States to our present condition. It is not, however, the men and women who make up the citizenry of America, the constituency of those who lead the nation, who have raised the cry for return to the fleshpots. It is and has been the leaders in the social order themselves, the possessors of intellectual and moral authority, who have blinded themselves to the truths of their heritage and rejected the moral responsibility of freedom. They have confused and bewildered those to whom it is their duty to give guidance and leadership. But the old truths, the old understanding still live in the hearts, the basic moral instincts, the fundamental beliefs of ordinary Americans. The established leaders can make them feel ashamed, ignorant, "backward," but they have not been able to eradicate their essential soundness.

The right instincts are there, the energy is there. For the shackling of Leviathan, the limitation of the state's invasion of the free domain of individual persons, those instincts await only intellectual articulation, that energy needs only organization. Here lies the challenge to resurgent conservatism in

America: simultaneously to create a new intellectual and spiritual leadership and on the basis of that leadership to move forward to the defeat of collectivist liberalism in the political sphere. Intellectually and spiritually it has twin tasks: to come to grips with and confute the prevailing relativist and positivist philosophy and to vindicate the great tradition of freedom of the person, exposing collectivist theory, however attenuated and whatever its source, in all its insidious menace. Politically, it must organize the power of the consensus of Americans to bring to the helm of the state men devoted to limiting the power of the state, to freeing the energies of individual persons from bureaucratic encroachment—and to directing the rightful power of the state against the ravening drive of the armed and messianic collectivism of Communism.

The issue rests upon the question: can the new and rising conservative leadership release and guide the pent-up energies, the intuitive understanding of their heritage, the love of freedom and virtue in the hearts of the American people, before the converging forces of cloying collectivism at home and armed collectivism abroad destroy the very meaning of freedom? That issue rests, as every important human issue always rests, in the hands of individual persons. Nothing in history is determined. The decision hangs upon our understanding of the tradition of Western civilization and the American republic, our devotion to freedom and to truth, the strength of our will and of our determination to live as free and virtuous men.

PART THREE

RELATED
ESSAYS

Why Freedom

I n reply to Brent Bozell's article, "Freedom or Virtue?" (Sept. 11), I should like first to plead innocent to his friendly indictment that I have "labored earnestly in recent years to promote and justify modern American conservatism as a 'fusion' of the libertarian and traditionalist points of view." Rather I (and others with whom I share a common outlook—he mentions Stanton Evans by name) have been attempting something very different from an ideological—and eclectic—effort to create a position abstractly "fusing" two other positions. What I have been attempting to do is to help articulate in theoretical and practical terms the instinctive consensus of the contemporary American conservative movement—a movement which is inspired by no ideological construct, but by devotion to the fundamental understanding of the men who made Western civilization and the American republic.

That consensus simultaneously accepts the existence of an objective moral and spiritual order, which places as man's end the pursuit of virtue, *and* the freedom of the individual person as a decisive necessity for a good political order. From the first of these principles it draws as corollaries its opposi-

Reprinted from *National Review* (September 25, 1962), 223–25, by permission. © 1962 by *National Review*, Inc., 150 East 35th Street, New York, NY 10016.

tion to positivism, relativism, and materialism; from the second, it draws its demand for principled limitation of the power of the state, for the strictest guarantees that the power of the state will be foreclosed from interference in the moral and spiritual sphere, in the economic sphere, or with the liberties of individual persons—so long as they do not by force or fraud coerce others.

That this double allegiance to virtue and to freedom is the overall consensus of contemporary American conservatism, the most cursory acquaintance with the conservative movement demonstrates. Mr. Bozell, I am sure, would agree that this is the actuality, no matter how much he may disapprove of it.

Every important publication of the movement exhibits the two motifs; so do the platforms of both conservative youth organizations, the Intercollegiate Society of Individualists and the Young Americans for Freedom; and the most widely read conservative book of the century, *The Conscience of a Conservative,* is an epitome of that unity.

Traditionalist and Libertarian

If I have "labored" to demonstrate the potential congruity of the "traditionalist" and "libertarian" positions, it has not been because I was "attempting to promote . . . a fusion," but because I have thought that the rigid positions of doctrinaire traditionalists and doctrinaire libertarians were both distortions of the same fundamental tradition and could be reconciled and assimilated in the central consensus of American conservatism. It is only when virtue or freedom is wrenched out of the intrinsic interdependence in which they have existed in our tradition that ideological opposition arises.

I have recently dealt in these pages with some of the results that occur when virtue is denied as an end for men and freedom raised to the sole end of man's existence. In "The Twisted Tree of Liberty"(*National Review*, Jan. 16), I tried to demonstrate that freedom, essential though it is as a condition for the virtuous life, is by itself without content or purpose if the existence of an objective moral order which men should strive to understand and move towards is not accepted. The results of such ideological abstraction of freedom from its functional foundation in the human condition are observable again and again as the pure libertarian develops his position—in the craven retreat before Communist tyranny of the pure libertarian of the nuclear-pacifist breed, as in the arid subhuman image of man and the calculated cruelties of Ayn Rand.

If, on the other hand, freedom is denied as a necessary condition of a good political order and the state is endowed with the right to enforce virtue upon individual persons, a parallel distortion occurs. Virtue, which is only virtue when freely chosen (this Mr. Bozell at bottom admits—as, being a Christian, he must admit), is made inaccessible to the coerced citizen, wherever and to the degree that the state compels his action. His actions may look like virtuous actions, but they are the actions of an automaton and cannot be truly virtuous, because being unfree to reject virtue, he is unfree to choose it. Even this assumes, however, that the men who hold the power of the state will use that power to enforce actions that are the simulacrum of virtue. But Lord Acton's insight still remains true, that there is in power a tendency to corrupt, and the more absolute the power, the more absolute the corruption. The experience of mankind has demonstrated this sad truth, however different may have been the philosophical foundations of those who held power that approached the absolute. Diocletian and Constantine, Inquisitionist and Cromwellian, Nazi and Communist—all have exhibited the corruption that power brings in its train. Each had a vision of how men ought to live and was determined to force that vision upon those subject to their will.

If the state is endowed with the power to enforce virtue, the men who hold that power will enforce their own concepts as virtuous.

Theocracy

Such a state of affairs is the opposite pole from—and as great a distortion as—the anarchistic worship of freedom as an absolute good without purpose or end. It is theocracy. That is, it is giving to some men the right and the power to enforce upon other men their own particular, limited, and perforce distorted, finite view of the Infinite—of God's will. And this remains true whether their God is the pagan god of Diocletian, or the Christian God of Constantine, Philip II, and Cromwell, or the *Volk* of the Nazis, or the dialectical materialist history of the Communists.

Mr. Bozell denies that his is a theocratic outlook, and indeed the positions he has taken in practice are far from theocratic, far from authoritarian. But the theoretical presuppositions put forward in "Freedom or Virtue?" nevertheless lead directly to theocracy. Whenever he wishes to justify his accord with practical measures conducive to freedom, he falls back upon the safeguards of "prudence." In *his* prudence I would have great confidence, but prudence is an art inherent in the men who exercise it. To hope that the men who exercise theocratic power will be prudent is a slender reed on which to base the defense of the freedom integrally necessary to a virtuous society.

For men imbued with the certainty of their vision of reality it will always be difficult to restrain the temptation to enforce that vision upon others and thus to derive them of the right freely to choose the good. It is the glory of Western civilization, with its Christian understanding of the shimmering tension between freedom and virtue, that it has in its essence held firm to its insistence upon both—although to the doggedly rational mind, the paradox of virtue in freedom is as much "a folly to the Greeks and a scandal to the Jews" as the Incarnation itself, which is the ground from which the strength to hold this paradoxical belief proceeds.

Christian Humanism and Positive Virtue

Mr. Bozell attacks "humanism" as the sin which pervades the belief in freedom, but there is a humanism implicit in the glorification of man by the Incarnation. It is his rejection of the humanist element in the Western and Christian tradition that leads Mr. Bozell to his insistence upon the radical opposition of the good society to the free society. The humanist side of that tradition has always held in check the Puritanical and Jansenist drive towards a conception of man as a totally corrupt creature. Realizing his tendencies towards corruption, the balanced tradition of the West has seen him at the same time as a son of God, who by the aid of grace and of the reason implanted in him possesses the highest of potentialities.

Therefore, it has conceived virtue not merely in the negative terms of subduing evil inclinations, but also in positive terms— in terms of achievement of potentialities which, although finite, are immeasurably great. Rejecting the Manichean disdain for the things of this world, it has considered the joy of created being as a high good. Its concept of virtue is positive, the performing of acts honorable, noble, valorous, glorious, generous. The free law of love is its highest command, not the meticulous performance of scheduled actions, the chalking up of gold stars and black marks in the records of a Divine Scorer.

Freedom, then, is a necessary political condition of a virtuous society, not only because the high likelihood is that the standards imposed by men with the power of the state would not in fact be virtuous standards, but also because, even if they were virtuous, to impose them upon individual persons would immensely reduce their ability to act virtuously at all and absolutely destroy their potentiality for active, creative, positive virtue.

Political Freedom

The key to the preservation of freedom is the limitation of the state. Political freedom can be defined as freedom from coercion in life, limb, liberty, or property by force or fraud; it has nothing to do with the ideas, the persuasions, the customs which go into forming every human person. To refuse to see, as Mr. Bozell seems to do, the differences between coercive acts against the person and the civilizational influences which help to form the person is to deny the difference between the authoritarian imposition of human power and the persuasive authority of truth and good.

Furthermore, political freedom has no relation to the definition Mr. Bozell imposes upon the libertarian conservative, that is, "the freedom to participate in the making of public policy." This is emphatically *not* what is meant by political freedom. What is meant by political freedom is the limitation of the power of the state to the function of preserving a free order. It demands that the state be prohibited from positive actions affecting the lives of individual persons, except insofar as such action is necessary to prevent the freedom of some from being exercised to limit the freedom of others.

Political freedom emphatically has nothing to do with who governs or who chooses the governors, but only with the strict limitation of the powers of the governors, whoever they may be.

The contradiction which Mr. Bozell posits between "political freedom" and "economic freedom" is a contradiction created out of his own misunderstanding. The freedom of the economic sphere from state interference is but one aspect of the freedom of persons in other spheres of their life from state interference. It is not possible for men to "exercise their political freedom against their economic freedom," as Mr. Bozell maintains; it is only possible for an overweening state to exercise its power against men's free activities in the economic sphere. A free economy is a condition of political freedom because it is an aspect of political freedom—exactly as are freedom of persons in their daily lives, freedom of thought and press and speech, freedom of worship.

The Triple Functions of a Limited State

If the goal of a free political order is accepted, there is no mystery of the sort Mr. Bozell professes to find in the principle that the state should be limited to the triple functions of defense against foreign enemies, preservation of internal order, and the administration of justice between man and man.

In fact, the derivation of this proposition is really no mystery to Mr. Bozell, as he makes clear a few lines later. He knows that it can be derived when freedom *is* considered as a political end, and certainly he is right that it could never be derived when society is considered as an "organism," of which men are cells. But to clear up whatever "mystery" there may be, I shall here briefly summarize how it is derived when men are thought of as persons for whom political freedom is morally vital. (For a further and more exhaustive consideration, I refer him, and any other readers who may be interested, to my book, *In Defense of Freedom: A Conservative Credo*, which will be published next month.)

Briefly, then: (1) There is great danger to human freedom, and thereby to the achievement of virtue, if any more power than that which is absolutely necessary is lodged in the same set of hands. (2) The state is a necessity as an institution to preserve the freedom of men from infringement by other men through domestic or foreign force or fraud and to settle the disputes that occur when rights clash with rights. (3) From this necessity are derived the legitimate powers of the state: defense, the preservation of domestic order, the administration of justice. (4) The exercise, however, of these necessary functions requires a dangerous concentration of power—the monopoly of legally and socially accepted force. Any additional control over individual persons in any sphere of their lives adds dangerously to this already dangerous concentration of power. (5) No other activities of men, except these three legitimate functions of the state, require the monopoly of force. All others can be performed by individual persons and voluntary associations of persons. (6) Since the power of the state is dangerous to begin with, and since all other functions beyond its essential three can be performed by men otherwise, the preservation of a truly free political order demands the limitation of the state to these functions.

To summarize: The principle that the political order must be a free order if men are to have the maximum possibilities of achieving virtue is, I maintain, inextricably linked, in the tradition of the West and the tradition of the American republic, with the principle that the goal of men is virtue. They are both essential principles of conservatism—which by definition is devoted to the preservation, maintenance, and extension of that tradition. Conservatism, therefore, unites the "traditionalist" emphasis upon virtue and the "libertarian" emphasis upon freedom. The denial of the claims of virtue leads not to conservatism, but to spiritual aridity and social anarchy; the denial of the claims of freedom leads not to conservatism, but to authoritarianism and theocracy.

When these attitudes are only emphases, differences of stress among conservatives, they can produce a fruitful and healthy dialogue. But neither the libertarian nor the traditionalist can totally deny the ends of the other without moving outside the conservative dialogue and breaking continuity with the Western tradition. That tradition bears onward from generation to generation the understanding—rooted in the Christian vision of the nature and destiny of man—of the primary value, under God, of the individual person. From his nature arises his duty to virtue and his inalienable right to freedom as a condition of the pursuit of virtue.

Neither virtue nor freedom alone, but the ineluctable combination of virtue *and* freedom is the sign and spirit of the West.

The West is in decay not, as Mr. Bozell asserts, because "the free society has come to take priority over the good society" but because freedom has declined as virtue has declined. The recovery of the one demands the recovery of the other; the recovery of both is the mission of conservatism today. *Virtue in freedom*—this is the goal of our endeavor.

In Defense of
John Stuart Mill

It is an unfortunate result of the quasi monopoly of the
major organs of discussion held by the collectivist Liberals
for the past generation that those who hold to the great
tradition of Western civilization have been deprived of the
means to carry on the dialectic between the different strands
of that tradition. Inhibited by the lack of a forum and also by
an understandable reluctance to divert energy from the primary endeavor of resisting the marshaled hosts of error, we
have tended to gloss over differences, the clarification of which
can only strengthen our common purpose and enrich the tradition for which we stand.

For that tradition is not a monolithic "party line." Its very
existence takes the form, in large part, of a long discourse between man and man and between God and man. The maintenance of that tradition requires a continuation of discourse,
pursued with respect for the accumulated wisdom of the past
and with responsibility towards the dictates of reason. Such discourse strives towards Truth with the humility to realize that
while Truth is objective and eternal, the quest for it by man's
finite understanding is unending; that while Truth is not avail-

Reprinted from *National Review* (March 28, 1956), 23–24, by permission.
© 1956 by *National Review*, Inc., 150 East 35th Street, New York, NY 10016.

able anew to each generation and each man, independent of the support of tradition, neither has it been at some point in the past given once and for all, so that there is nothing left to do but pass it on from generation to generation.

Thus, as we approach the one hundredth anniversary of the publication of John Stuart Mill's *On Liberty*, I would maintain against the view of Russell Kirk (*National Review*, January 25) that the aspect of the nineteenth century which that book reflects—its character as an Age of Discussion and its love of liberty—is the respect in which it is most glorious and most resembles such high points in man's strivings as fifth-century Athens and thirteenth-century Christendom. This is not to defend the materialism and scientism of the nineteenth century, any more than to salute John Stuart Mill's defense of liberty is to overlook the confusion and errors of his philosophical position. But it seems to me that Mr. Kirk attacks both Mill and the Victorian Age for those qualities from which we have the most to learn and which, despite all the shortcomings of the man and the age, we must cherish against the blank conformity and power idolatry of our day. Likewise, from Mill's antagonist, the complex James Fitzjames Stephen, he appears to select for praise those ideas which Stephen's imagination drew from the Romantic pagan-Teutonic mystique of folk, community, force, and power. All too familiar, they presage the nightmares of the twentieth century, with which the nineteenth century was so sadly pregnant.

Both Mill and Stephen were nurtured in the bosom of utilitarianism, a position not only philosophically unsound, but also historically disastrous in its effects; nor did either of them ever free himself from its influences. Nothing in the writings of Bentham or either of the Mills, it seems to me, is any more blatantly utilitarian than Stephen's discussion of liberty, which Mr. Kirk adduces in condemnation of Mill:

> To me the question whether liberty is a good or a bad thing appears as irrational as the question whether fire is a good or a bad

thing? It is both good and bad according to time, place, and circumstance. . . .

Mr. Kirk himself, after all, calls liberty "the quality which, after divine grace and right reason, lifts man above the brutes." Surely, such a quality cannot be considered "both good and bad, according to time, place, and circumstance." And if it might seem that I am drawing a strained implication from Stephen's words, to confirm its cogency it is only necessary to dip at random into his answer to Mill's essay, his *Liberty, Equality, Fraternity*, an essay that glorifies force and power against reason and moral truth. The most fundamental questions of right and truth are reduced to a calculus of power:

> Is there or not a God and a future state? . . . the attitude of the law and of public authority generally towards the discussion of this question will and *ought* to depend upon the nature of the view which happens to be dominant for the time being on the question itself. . . . [my emphasis]

Despite Utilitarianism

Granted that the foundations of Mill's position are no less utilitarian than Stephen's. Granted that with him, as with Stephen, morality is equated with utility until, strictly considered, the very possibility of standards by which experience is to be judged and conduct inspired is swept away. Granted, in short, that for many of the most powerful minds and spirits of the mid-nineteenth century, the tradition of the West lay in a pile of shattered debris. The fact remains that John Stuart Mill was one of the first to challenge the impending results of the tidal wave that had been set in motion; to struggle mightily, in his own way, as R. P. Anschutz has shown in *The Philosophy of John Stuart Mill*, with the doctrines in which he had been raised. It is true that he never succeeded in breaking loose from that barren system; but in vindicating the individual person as the measure of value over against the collective instrumentalities of state and society and in demanding that the worth of a society should be judged by the degree to which it makes possible the freedom of the individual, he vindicated the first principle of morality (for no man can act morally unless he is free to choose good from evil). He posited against the state centralism that was developing along with unrestricted and total democracy the fundamental social and political derivative of the natural law: the inalienable rights of the individual.

His fault is not in his conclusions, but in his mode of arriving at them. He did not understand the source of man's rights in the realm of value beyond history. A fundamental philosophical error, which is the essential error of utilitarianism, of positivism, of all monism, vitiates his thought: the confusion of fact and value, the erection of man's history into a standard by which that history is to be judged. As Eric Voegelin in *The New Science of Politics* and Percy of Newcastle in *The Heresy of Democracy* have both in their different ways so cogently demonstrated, this is an error which has possessed a large section of Western thought—theist as well as atheist, conservative as well as radical—to the great detriment of the wisdom and peace of our civilization. To be sure, it has been possible, as we have seen over and over again, for noble minds to cling to false systems and to make nevertheless substantial intellectual contributions. Men—even philosophers—do not always think with logical rigor. More streams than one enter their consciousness and help to form their product. Edmund Burke, for example, whose thinking was corrupted through and through with this historicist, expediential outlook (one which, as Richard Weaver has demonstrated, showed through his very rhetoric), played a glorious role during one of the greatest crises in the history of the West.

Might or Right?

To attack Mill for his philosophical errors, even to stress the decisive effect which in his case those errors had at an important moment in the development of thought, is legitimate enough and in fact of great value in clarifying some of the most confused issues of the day. To condemn him, however, not as having unsound foundations for his defense of liberty, but for that defense itself; to champion against him an antagonist as unsound as Mill philosophically, as utilitarian as Mill himself, one who can be caught blatantly attacking the ideal of the freedom of the person through glorification of the sword; to hold that the triumph of the mailed tyrannies of the twentieth century "refutes" and "dates" Mill's ringing vindication of liberty: this, it seems to me, is to put forward the claims of power over spirit, blind force over right reason, matter over man, what is over what ought to be.

The basis of Mill's defense of the liberty of the individual is unsound not because the liberty of the individual is anything less than the first (although not the only) political principle of a good society and certainly not because the victory of totalitarianism and welfarism in the twentieth century makes liberty an "outdated" ideal; it is unsound because the grounds of his defense, far from being too absolute, are not absolute enough and, secondarily, because of the unclarity of his concept of society and his tendency to equate society with the state.

I am myself prepared to defend a position more absolute than Mill's, because I assert the right of individual freedom not on the grounds of utility but on the grounds of the very nature of man and the nature of the drama of his existence. He lives between good and evil, beauty and ugliness, truth and error, and he fulfills his destiny in the choices he makes. No social institution, not even the conglomerate of such institutions we call for convenience "society," can make the least one of these choices. In that sense they are neither free nor unfree. Only the individual person, whose fate it is to choose, can be free, for freedom is no more nor less than the possibility—and responsibility—to choose. Freedom is the essence of the being of man, and since all social institutions are subordinate to men, the virtue of political and social institutions should be judged by the degree to which they expand or contract the area of freedom. Force, which Mr. Kirk, with Stephen, seems to regard as the great mover of history that confounds reasonable discussion and refutes the ideal of liberty, surely has no moral character of its own. It is controlled by men, for evil or for good; and the ideal of the utmost liberty for each individual man to make his choice is the end to which force should be directed. It is in this sense that Mill's championship of the individual against the state and society must, I believe, be accepted as an important part of our heritage.

Conservatism and Liberty

The only alternative to the moral rule of liberty of the individual is to enthrone the sad tendency of human history as right, to glorify with James Stephen "the man of genius who rules by persuading an efficient minority to coerce an indifferent and self-indulgent majority. . . ." The use of force against those who propound error is wrong, not because it is inexpedient but because it is an outrage upon the freedom of man and, in that, upon the very nature of man. Liberty is the political end of man's existence because liberty is the condition of his being. It is for this reason that conservatism, which in preserving the tradition preserves this truth, is only constant to itself when it is libertarian.

Conservatives
in Pursuit of Truth

A correspondent in the May 16 issue of *National Review,* commenting upon Russell Kirk's article on John Stuart Mill and my rejoinder thereto, raises an issue of the most serious moment. My difference of opinion with Mr. Kirk on the place of the concept of liberty in political thought, he sees as representing a "fundamental—and irreconcilable— ideological division among those who call themselves conservatives."

That this issue is fundamental I agree, but I do not think it is irreconcilable. There is no question but that in the ranks of those who are dedicated to the conservation and revitalization of the great tradition of the West, there exist diverse emphases upon different aspects of that tradition. More particularly, there is a very sharp division between those who emphasize continuity and authority and those who emphasize reason and the autonomy of the person as the basis of their opposition to the prevailing relativism and value nihilism, collectivism, and statism. But these emphases are not irreconcilable, even if they are sometimes so one-sided as to lose sight of their mutual interdependence.

Reprinted from *National Review* (June 6, 1956), 16, by permission. © 1956 by *National Review,* Inc., 150 East 35th Street, New York, NY 10016.

The one emphasis, traditionalist and authoritative, stressing the values expressed and maintained in the tradition of Western and Christian civilization, tends to regard economic and political forms as comparatively unimportant, and to underestimate a great insight of that tradition, that those values cannot be compelled, that they can only be freely chosen by each individual person. Or, to the degree that it does recognize the importance of freedom, it tends to assume that freedom will automatically prevail and that the economic and political forms necessary to safeguard it will spontaneously arise if only the moral ends of human existence and the traditional prescriptions in which they are incorporated are maintained. Deeply aware that truth and good are the ends of man's existence, it too easily loses sight of the essential condition of man's pursuit of those ends: he cannot choose the good and the true unless he is free to choose, and that must mean as free to reject as to accept.

The Other Extreme

The other emphasis, individualist and libertarian, puts at the center of its consideration the prime *condition* of the search for truth: freedom. Concerned by the fearful threat to the pursuit of value that concentrated power constitutes, particularly under the circumstances of modern technology, it stresses the political and economic prerequisites of freedom. It insists upon the limitation of the state to its essential functions of defense, the preservation of order, and the administration of justice and upon the untrammeled operation of a capitalist market economy as the incommutable foundations of that freedom in an industrial society.

Concentrating upon the safeguards of freedom and the power of reason to arrive at any understanding of freedom, it sometimes tends to forget that reason is well-grounded only when it operates within tradition, that is, in the light of the accumulated wisdom of the generations; and, in its concern with the preservation of the freedom of the individual person, it can lose sight of the philosophical values which are at the same time the ends which freedom serves and the very foundation of that respect for the innate dignity of the individual person upon which the defense of freedom rests.

Although these two emphases in conservative thought can and do pull away from each other, and although there is serious danger of their so doing when the proponents of either forsake their common heritage of belief in immutable value as man's proper end and his freedom under God as the condition of the achievement of his end, it is precisely because they mutually possess that very heritage that their division is not "irreconcilable." Extremists on one side may look with equanimity upon the recrudescence of an authoritarian status society if only it promulgates the doctrines in which they believe. Extremists on the other side may care not what becomes of ultimate values if only their political and economic individualism prevails. But both extremes are self-defeating: truth withers when freedom dies, however righteous the authority that kills it; and free individualism uninformed by moral value rots at its core and soon surrenders to tyranny.

A Confusion of Levels

Such extremes are not the necessary outcome of the principled pursuit of the truth. Discussion or dialectic between different emphases based upon the same fundamental understanding is the mode by which finite men have achieved much of the wisdom contained in tradition. Through it they can attain today a common position to which "the wise and the honest may repair"—if only the protagonists, in pressing that aspect of the truth which they regard as decisive, do not totally exclude from their consideration other and complementary aspects of the same truth.

The essence of the problem is, in my opinion, the confusion of the metaphysical with the moral-political levels. Thus, the aforementioned correspondent accuses me of being "in love with the 'freedom to choose,' not with the truth that that freedom may lead to." But the point is that the "truth" is a *metaphysical end* and "the freedom to choose" is, so far as human beings are concerned, the *moral-political condition* of achieving that end.

There is no more logic in the conclusion that a love of freedom implies a disbelief in, a lack of enthusiasm for, ultimate values than there is in the Liberal canard that a belief in ultimate values makes impossible a belief in freedom. The reverse is the case: the belief in ultimate values and the belief in freedom are dependent one upon the other, integral aspects of the same understanding. The love of liberty and the love of truth are not the hostile standards of irreconcilable parties; rather they form together the twin sign of any viable conservatism.

Conservatism and Crisis:
A Reply to Father Parry

Them here is a sense in which Disraeli's dictum on "the two nations" is true of the United States today. But it is true not in Disraeli's—or in Karl Marx's—sense of a profound gulf between a poor and frustrated majority and a powerful and wealthy minority. The opposition between "the two nations" that constitute the United States today is characterized by spiritual and intellectual differences, not by differences of wealth and economic power.

A profound chasm has come into being between the beliefs and instincts of the solid citizenry of the country and the ideology of the dominant section of those whose powers and talents determine the tone and direction of our national life. For some decades now, the tradition of Western civilization—both generally and in its specific American form—has been under concerted attack from a corrosive and nihilistic ideology, which has perversely seized upon the century's broadening in factual knowledge as a charter for frontal attack upon the age-old wisdom of the civilization concerning the nature and destiny of men. Positivist in its epistemology, relativist in its ontology (if ontology is a proper category for such metaphysical nihilism), Utopian, to the point of *hubris* and beyond, in its conviction

Reprinted from *Modern Age* (Winter 1962–63): 45–50, by permission.

that human beings can be manipulated and "structured" like beams of steel to satisfy an engineer's blueprint, this ideology takes political form in what today is called Liberalism.

It is this outlook which characterizes the presently predominant intellectual and governmental leadership of the nation. But, although that leadership maintains itself in power upon the basis of a quasi-monopolistic control of the channels of communication and by proposing speciously attractive programs, appealing to apparent immediate interests of sections of the electorate, it has not succeeded in seriously establishing its ideology in the minds and souls of the American people.

"Civilizational Crisis"?

Making free with Toynbee's phrases, I would maintain that there is indeed a "schism in the body politic," but that there is not so far in the generality of Americans a "schism in the soul." It is here that I would begin to take exception to Father Stanley Parry's consideration of the present state of our society ("The Restoration of Tradition," *Modern Age,* Spring 1961).

His analysis of the forms of social crisis is brilliant. In particular, his discussion of the deepest form of social crisis, what he calls "civilizational crisis," is profound and accurate; but I challenge his premise that we in the United States are in the grip of a crisis of this type. Such a crisis Father Parry defines as involving "a falling out of the area of experience of large segments of previously held truth"—that is, the destruction of fundamental traditional beliefs in the minds of the people who make up the civilization.

No one can deny, of course, that the impact of the views and attitudes of the intellectual leadership has affected and distorted the form in which traditional truths are held and understood by the American people; but all evidence points to the essential survival of that tradition in the *ethos* of the people.

And when I say "the people," I do not mean only "the man on the street"; I mean also the great majority of professionals and businessmen and community leaders, of Congressmen and state senators and legislators and municipal officials. The other "nation," powerful though it is, is a limited and shallow stratum; sometimes described as the Liberal Establishment, it is constantly horrified and constantly thwarted by the refusal of the solid strata of American society to acquiesce in its outlook. To give but a few random examples: its "sophisticated" moves towards appeasement of Communism have brought into existence a widespread and deeply rooted anti-Communist movement; its flossy "educational" projects—projects without substance and totally unrelated to true education—are being defeated in bond vote after bond vote in communities all over the country; the socializing projects of the bureaucracy and the Executive again and again are thwarted by the Congress; and, most offensive to the Establishment, a strong and solid conservatism with firm intellectual foundations is arising to challenge it at every level of American life.

These are not the symptoms of a dying civilization. This is not Father Parry's "change in the very structure of the community's experience of truth in history." This is not Toynbee's "schism in the soul"; it is more akin to Spengler's figure of "pseudomorphosis." The essential health of the American tradition remains vigorously alive; but it is imprisoned in the mould that a dominant Liberalism has for a time succeeded in imposing upon it. Whatever the case may be in the other provinces of Western civilization, in the United States our crisis is not of the "dissolution" of tradition; it is a crisis brought about by the sad fact that those whose duty it is to articulate the tradition have betrayed it. Our crisis calls not for a new concept of truth to form a new tradition, but for intellectual, moral, and political leaders who can articulate again and develop in contemporary terms a tradition that in its essence is still doggedly defended by the people.

Is Conservatism Relevant?

Therefore, the opposition of conservatism and Liberalism is not, as Father Parry maintains, irrelevant to the decisive issue; it *is* the issue. Were our crisis a "civilizational crisis" in his sense, a deep-going "change from order and truth to disorder and negation," a change shared in by the whole of society, then it would be true that conservatism is simply a "formula for escaping inevitabilities in history." For then the conservative effort to vindicate the fundamental spirit and understanding of our civilization, its "shared participation of truth," would be meaningless. If the civilization were indeed so dead in the hearts of the people, then the only adequate response *would* be to drive free of the civilizational debris and devote all energies to proclaiming the essential truths of man's good in timeless terms, without respect or piety towards the shaped forms and the rich heritage in which, as citizens of Christendom and of the American republic, our understanding of truth lives.

If this were so, then Father Parry's "prophetic response," not conservatism, would be the stance of a man who was a man. There are times when so deeply revolutionary a response *is* demanded—for the "prophetic response" is a revolutionary response. It challenges not merely the perversions and distortions of truth which have grown up in the civilization's perception of truth and in its body politic, but it challenges the very form the civilization's perception of truth has taken. It says, not only that the vision of the civilization has been perverted, but that at its best it has become outmoded before a higher vision; that its very way of understanding and of guiding human life is no longer a way to truth and good, but has become an inhibiting limitation upon the spirit.

It is true that the prophetic *tone* has many levels. And when the conservative movement is embarked upon the course of combat against the perversion of a civilization, upon the course of restoring the civilization, that tone may well be necessary. There is something of the revolutionary, or, if you wish, counterrevolutionary, in the endeavor to wipe out the perversion of a civilization, to return to the source of its virtue, to reassert and bring to fruition its pristine glory. But it is not in this sense that Father Parry, following Eric Voegelin, writes of "prophetic response." He means (this is why he regards the conservative enterprise as irrelevant) that our civilization has passed the point of no return. It has, to use his phrase, "fallen out of existence."

While I will not deny that such things have happened in history—to Sumeria, to Egypt, to the Classical world—I do not believe that Western Christendom has run its course. Whatever may be in store for it in the European land of its birth, I do not believe that in the United States, the most forward thrust and strongest bastion of the West, thirty years of Karl Marx, John Dewey, and Franklin Roosevelt have cast us adrift, "out of existence" in a civilizationless void.

The Relevance of Conservatism

Therefore, the contemporary American conservative effort is far from irrelevant. Rather it is directed with precision towards overcoming the actual spiritual, moral, and political crisis we do face today—not Father Parry's systemic "civilizational crisis," but a schism in our society between the outlook, the "perception of truth," of those who hold decisive political and ideological power and that of the people as a whole. Having said this, I must add that a "civilizational crisis" in Father Parry's terms is not impossible in the not-too-distant future; if the leadership of our society remains much longer in the hands of those who hold it today, it is possible that they will succeed in totally destroying the Western consciousness, the instinct for virtue and freedom, which still informs the *ethos* of Americans beyond the direct influence of the Establishment.

The problem can be stated in the starkest terms: Can the men of the rising conservative movement in America expel the dominant Establishment from its positions of control before they succeed in bringing about the corruption of the American people in the image of their own corruption?

This is not simply—perhaps not primarily—a political problem. It is a confrontation at every level: intellectual, moral, social, political. The conservative task would seem to be a heroic task. All the heights of our society—with the partial exception of the Congress and the state legislatures—are occupied by forces inspired by a Liberalism philosophically nihilistic to the genius of Western civilization. That task would be more than heroic, it would be a valiant but hopeless Lost Cause, were it not that the attacking conservative forces can draw upon the energies and vitality of those who make up the body of the social order.

The Place of Freedom

Father Parry's insistence upon the deep and final character of the crisis of our civilization and his insistence upon the irrelevance of the conservative-Liberal polarity stems, I believe, from his failure to understand the specific genius of Western civilization which inspired our Constitution and the men who created it and guided the Republic in its early years. They created a political instrumentality congruent with the deep Western fusion of belief in the authority of absolute truth and good with belief in the dignity and freedom of the individual person. This was an epochal leap forward in the development of the Western and Christian vision of the majesty of God and the freedom of man. Father Parry condemns the contemporary American conservative devotion to this breathtaking vision of human potentiality under God (he calls it "spiritual individualism") as a hopeless and fatal "refusal to consider the issue of substantive truth." He ranges it alongside of Liberalism and reaction and economism as a "partial response" to our crisis— a response doomed to disaster because it does not come to grips with the truth of the human condition.

He fails completely to understand that the great social and political problem of Western civilization—how to establish an order that makes possible the flowering of devotion to truth and good and simultaneously preserves the freedom of the individual person—is here solved in principle for the first time. The key is the limitation of the power of the state—that is, of the power of some men to impose their beliefs on other men— while to the natural leaders of the social order is given the duty of leading and persuading their fellow men in the paths of justice and truth. Where has there ever been a society at once so noble and so free as the American republic in the first half century of its existence? And what destroyed the promise of that idyllic spring but the successive infringements upon the concept of divided and limited governmental power, which are historically symbolized (each time more catastrophically) by the development of mass democratism in the 1830s, by the undermining of the sovereignty of the several states in the 1860s, and by the naturalization in this country of the theory and practice of the twentieth-century collectivism in the 1930s?

Because Father Parry conceives freedom only as a by-product, not as a primary condition, of a good social order, he does not understand the character of the sickness of our society: the displacement of freedom in behalf of what those with power think the good to be. It does not matter here that I would agree with Father Parry that their concept of the good is disastrously wrong, totally out of accord with the constitution of being; the evidence of historical experience confirms what the founders of the Republic drew from the insight of the West: if the freedom of individual persons is not guaranteed by the arrangements of the political order, power always corrupts, even when the motives of those who use it to enforce their beliefs are beneficent. This is not to deny the necessity of devotion to virtue in the persons who make up a social order, and particularly in those who hold positions of influence in it, if such an order is to survive. But to affirm the necessity of virtue as an end for men does not require the subordination of freedom. Rather, if individual persons, who are the only spiritually significant entities in the social order, are to achieve virtue, they must be free. The responsibility for recognizing the demands of virtue, articulating the modes of virtue, and inculcating virtue cannot rest in any social organism, but only in individual persons. The coercive organs of society cannot establish or enforce virtue, since by its nature virtue must be the free choice of persons. The attempt to enforce it by power turns gold into dross.

The Vision of the West

The deep understanding that the Founders of our Republic derived from the essential Christian and Western recognition of the mutual independence of virtue and freedom, they made socially actual in the institutions and the *ethos* of the Republic. Father Parry rejects that high point in Western history; he maintains that to posit virtue and freedom as interdependent necessities of the social order and to place the responsibility for virtue upon the individual is to neglect "the problem of right social order and in doing so [to neglect] the central problem of civilizational crisis." But this "spiritual individualism" *is* our tradition. It is this understanding that still remains in the hearts of the American people, inarticulate, instinctive perhaps, but firmly held. And it is to the articulation, the renewal, the development in contemporary conditions of their vision that the rising American conservative leadership is devoted.

There is no certainty that this leadership will in sufficient time achieve the intellectual and political victory necessary to insure the triumph of the spirit of Western civilization it embodies. But if it does not, that will be its failure; it will not be because it has embarked upon a hopeless endeavor. For the

West is not dead in spirit; its glorious vision—the highest ever achieved by men—remains.

It is not only from the collectivist riders of power abroad and at home that defeat can come. The tenuous tension between the claims of virtue and the claims of freedom can be upset as well by men who—although they hate tyranny and collectivism with a fierce hatred—blind themselves to the central truth of the West, that neither virtue nor freedom can be made the end in a social order at the expense of the other without spiritual disaster.

Father Parry's Spenglerian pessimism on the fate of Western civilization rests on other foundations than Spengler's own; and he, basing himself upon a Rock firmer than any civilization, has hope, where Spengler had only grim fortitude. Civilizations have been born and civilizations have died; and it may be that ours will turn out to have been at the point of death in this mid-twentieth century. But whether this will be so or not depends upon our understanding and our energies. It depends upon our strength to recover the essence of our past, upon the imagination and vigor with which we can create the forms in which that essence can be realized under contemporary conditions. It depends upon the stamina and the courage we can summon to fight for the Western vision against the perversions that assail us from every side.

We may, I repeat, be defeated. But only then—after we have tried with our deepest energies to vindicate the truths of the West, when in our defeat the Western forms of truth no longer live in the hearts of men—only then will Father Parry's "prophetic response" be the part required of men devoted to truth and good. That day has not come. The West still lives. Today our need is not for "prophets" in Father Parry's sense—men who, with everything destroyed behind them, delve deep into reality to reestablish a form for truth when all forms lie in shards. In every aspect of human endeavor—philosophical, social, political, military—what we need are fighters for the reasoned and revealed incarnation of truth, virtue, freedom that Western civilization has been and can again be.

Libertarianism or Libertinism?

T he development of contemporary American conservatism has been marked, on the theoretical level, by a
continuing tension between a traditionalist emphasis
and a libertarian emphasis. Over the years I have argued that
these positions are in fact not incompatible opposites, but complementary poles of a tension and balance which, both in theory and practice, define American conservatism as it has come
into being at midcentury. If anything, I have stressed the libertarian emphasis because I have felt that unmodified traditionalism, stressing virtue and order in disregard of the ontological
and social status of the freedom of the individual person,
tended dangerously towards an authoritarianism wrong in itself
and alien to the spirit of American conservatism.

Recently, however, there have been ominous signs that the
danger of a disbalance just as alien to conservatism is arising
not from traditionalist quarters, but from an untrammeled libertarianism, which tends as directly to anarchy and nihilism as
unchecked traditionalism tends to authoritarianism. This libertarianism can be seen at its most extreme in such dropouts
from the Right as Murray Rothbard and Karl Hess and their

Reprinted from *National Review* (September 9, 1969), 910, by permission.
© 1969 by *National Review*, Inc., 150 East 35th Street, New York, NY 10016.

handful of followers. While their position has become indistinguishable from that of the SDS, there are increasing signs of a more widespread, if more moderate, development in this direction, primarily among the young, but by no means restricted to them. The essential rationale of this position is so far removed from the rationale of libertarian conservatism and so completely ignores the proper foundations of liberty in the actual circumstances of the human condition that, like the position of the anarchist wing of the SDS, its proper denomination is not libertarianism but libertinism.

A true libertarianism is derived from metaphysical roots in the very constitution of being, and places its defense of freedom as a political end in the context of moral responsibility for the pursuit of virtue and the underlying social necessity for the preservation of order. The libertine impulse that masquerades as libertarianism, on the other hand, disregards all moral responsibility, ranges itself against the minimum needs of social order, and raises the freedom of the individual person (regarded as the unbridled expression of every desire, intellectual or emotional) to the status of an absolute end.

Libertine Ideologues

The underlying issue between conservative libertarianism and libertine libertarianism is at bottom a totally opposed view of the nature and destiny of men. The libertines—like those other products of the modern world, ritualistic liberals, socialists, Communists, fascists—are ideologues first and last. That is, they reject reality as it has been studied, grasped, understood, and acted upon in five thousand years or so of civilized history and pose an abstract construction as the basis of action. They would replace God's creation of this multifarious, complex world in which we live and substitute for it their own creation, simple, neat, and inhuman—as inhuman as the blueprints of the bulldozing engineer.

The place of freedom in the spiritual economy of men is a high one indeed, but it is specific and not absolute. By its very nature, it cannot be an end of men's existence. Its meaning is essentially freedom from coercion, but that, important as it is, cannot be an end. It is empty of goal or norm. Its function is to relieve men of external coercion so that they may freely seek their good.

It is for this reason that libertarian conservatives champion freedom as the end of the *political* order: politics, which is, at its core, the disposition of force in society, will, if not directed towards this end, create massive distortions and obstacles in men's search for their good. But that said, an equally important question remains. Free, how are men to use their freedom? The libertine answers that they should do what they want. Sometimes, in the line of the philosophers of the French Revolution, he arbitrarily posits the universal benevolence of human beings. He presumes that if everyone does whatever he wants, everything will be for the best in the best of all possible worlds. But whether so optimistically qualified or not, his answer ignores the hard facts of history. For it is only in civilization that men have begun to rise towards their potentiality; and civilization is a fragile growth, constantly menaced by the dark forces that suck man back towards his brutal beginnings.

Reason and Tradition

The essence of civilization, however, is tradition; no single generation of men can of itself discover the proper ends of human existence. At its best, as understood by contemporary American conservatism, the traditionalist view accepts political freedom, accepts the role of reason and innovation and criticism; but it insists, if civilization is to be preserved, that reason operate within tradition and that political freedom is only effectively achieved when the bulwarks of civilizational order are preserved.

Libertine libertarianism would shatter those bulwarks. In its opposition to the maintenance of defenses against Communism, its puerile sympathy with the rampaging mobs of campus and ghetto, its contempt for the humdrum wisdom of the great producing majority, it is directed towards the destruction of the civilizational order which is the only real foundation in a real world for the freedom it espouses. The first victim of the mobs let loose by the weakening of civilizational restraint will be, as it has always been, freedom—for anyone, anywhere.

Conservatism

To discuss conservatism in America today is to plunge at once into a tangle of semantic confusion. There have been over the past few years so many efforts, often contradictory, by scholars and journalists to extract its essence and define its limits that it is with some diffidence I begin with a rather broad and general description of it.

What Is Conservatism?

This essay is concerned with conservatism as a political, social, and intellectual movement—not as a cast of mind or a temperamental inclination. Such a movement arises historically when the unity and balance of a civilization are riven by revolutionary transformations of previously accepted norms of polity, society, and thought. Conservatism comes into being at such times as a movement of consciousness and action directed to recovering the tradition of the civilization. This is the essence of conservatism in all the forms it has assumed in different civilizations and under differing circumstances. Sometimes such

Reprinted from *Left, Right and Center: Essays on Liberalism and Conservatism in the United States*, ed. Robert A. Goldwin (Chicago: Rand McNally, for the Public Affairs Conference Center, Kenyon College, Gambier, Ohio, 1967), by permission.

movements are successful, as was the return to the basic Egyptian tradition after Akhenaton's revolutionary changes. Sometimes they succeed for a time and modulate the later and further development of the revolutionary impulse, as did the Stuart restoration after the English Revolution or the European consolidation after the French Revolution and the reign of Napoleon. Sometimes they have little effect on contemporary events but make a tremendous impress on the consciousness of the future, as did the Platonic reaction to the destruction of the balance of civilization brought about by the overweening power drive of the Athenian *demos* and the arrogance of Sophistical thought. Sometimes they fail utterly and are lost to history.

In any era the problem of conservatism is to find the way to restore the tradition of the civilization and apply it in a new situation. But this means that conservatism is by its nature two-sided. It must at one and the same time be reactionary and presentist. It cannot content itself with appealing to the past. The very circumstances that call conscious conservatism into being create an irrevocable break with the past. The many complex aspects of the past had been held together in tension by the unity of the civilization, but that particular tension, that particular suspension in unity, can never be re-created after a revolutionary break. To attempt to re-create it would be pure unthinking reaction (what Toynbee calls "archaism") and would be bound to fail; nor could reaction truly restore the civilizational tradition to the recovery of which it was putatively directed. But while conservatism is not and cannot be naked reaction, neither can its concern with contemporary circumstances lead it, if it is to be true to itself, to be content with the status quo, with serving as a "moderating wing" within the existing situation. For that situation is the result of a revolutionary break with the tradition of the civilization, and to "conserve" it is to accept the radical break with tradition that conservatism exists to overcome.

Conservatism is neither reactionary yearning for an irreme-
diably lost past, nor is it trimming acquiescence in the consolidation of revolution, just so long as the revolution does not go
too fast. It is a vindication and renewal of the civilizational tradition as the fundament upon which reason must build to solve
the problems of the present.

It is absurd, therefore, because one conservative voice in one
period showed an underlying hostility to reason, to maintain,
as is today so often done, that Edmund Burke's attitude to reason is an essential element of any definition of conservatism.
True, no conservatism can accept utopian reliance upon the
limited reason of one generation (or one school of thought
within that generation), which ignores the tradition and builds
upon arrogant confidence in its own experience and its own
ratiocination. But conservatism is not antirational. It demands
only that reason operate upon the foundation of the tradition
of civilization, that is, upon the basis of the accumulated reason, experience, and wisdom of past generations.

From the point of view of contemporary "liberalism," it may
indeed seem that any respect for tradition is *ipso facto* a repudi-
ation of reason. This, together with the fact that Burke was to a
rather strong degree critical of the claims of reason and that
nineteenth-century conservatism often tended in this direction, may explain, although it does not excuse, the insistence
of author after author in late years (most recently, Morton
Auerbach in *The Conservative Illusion*) that no movement has a
right to the name of conservatism if it does not fit the mould of
an exaggerated representation of Burke's views on reason.
Thus, the contemporary American conservative movement has
consistently been denied its right to its self-chosen name by
critics who refuse to think deeply and seriously about the phenomenon of conservatism, preferring instead facilely to derive
their criteria from ephemeral characteristics of the conservatism of a single historical period.

It is easy to show that contemporary American conservatism

is not a replica of nineteenth-century European conservatism; while it resembles it in some ways, it also resembles nineteenth-century European liberalism in its commitment to individual liberty and its corollary commitment to an economic system free of state control. But to show that is to prove nothing of substance. The claim of the contemporary American conservative movement to the title conservative does not have to be based upon a surface resemblance to the conservative movement of another period. It is based upon its commitment to the recovery of a tradition, the tradition of Western civilization and the American republic, which has been subjected to a revolutionary attack in the years since 1932.

The Contemporary American Conservative Movement

The crystallization in the past dozen years or so of an American conservative movement is a delayed reaction to the revolutionary transformation of America that began with the election of Franklin Roosevelt in 1932. That revolution itself has been a gentler, more humane, bloodless expression in the United States of the revolutionary wave that has swept the globe in the twentieth century. Its grimmest, most total manifestations have been the phenomena of Communism and Nazism. In rather peculiar forms in late years it has expressed itself in the so-called nationalism typified by Nasser, Nkrumah, and Sukarno; in Western Europe it has taken the forms of the socialism of England or that of Scandinavia. Everywhere, however open or masked, it represents an aggrandizement of the power of the state over the lives of individual persons. Always that aggrandizement is cloaked in a rhetoric and a program putatively directed to and putatively concerned for "the masses."

The American form of that revolution differs little in its essentials from Western European democratic socialism. But, by an ironic twist of history, it has become known as "liberalism."

(So far is it removed from the classical liberalism of the nineteenth century, with its overriding concern for individual liberty and the limitation of the state, that clear discourse requires some mode of differentiation; and I shall for that reason, through the rest of this essay, refer to this twentieth-century American development as Liberalism, with a capital *L*, reserving the lowercase for classical liberalism.) Ushered in by the election of 1932, so thorough was the victory of Liberalism that for many years afterwards it met with no concerted resistance in either the intellectual or political sphere. True, islands of resistance remained—in the Congress, in the academy among some economists and humanists, in the business community, in the endemic mass anti-Communist movement among some strata of the population. These were rearguard actions; by and large, Liberalism dominated the scene, took over the academy and the organs of mass communication, controlled the Democratic party, and slowly penetrated the Republican party. Only in recent years has there emerged a consistent, cohesive conservative movement, based upon a broad consensus of principle, challenging Liberal assumptions and Liberal power all along the line.

In its intellectual origins, centered among a group of writers gathered around the old *Freeman, National Review,* and *Modern Age*, it early attracted a following and guided a movement in the universities, and gradually focused and channelized the energies of disparate tendencies opposed to Liberalism through all levels of society. During the past half dozen years its attitude began to be reflected among a group of young Congressmen, and it fully emerged on the national political arena with the nomination of Barry Goldwater at the Republican convention of 1964.

There are many strands in this movement, many trends in its thought. In particular there exists within it a continuing tension between an emphasis on tradition and virtue, on the one hand, and an emphasis on reason and freedom, on the other. I will return to this problem a little farther on; here I want only to say that these differences are but differences of emphasis, creating tensions within a common consensus, not sharply opposed points of view.

That common consensus of the contemporary American conservative movement is reflected, with different degrees of understanding and depth, at every level of the conservative movement. It underlies the principled positions of the consciously intellectual as it does the empirical positions and the instinctive attitudes of the political activists and the broad constituency of that movement. The clearest way, I think, to summarize this consensus is to contrast it with the beliefs and attitudes of the Liberal world outlook, which sets the prevailing tone of contemporary American society. I do not assert that every conservative accepts every one of the articles of belief I am positing or that every Liberal accepts each of the contrasted articles. But I would maintain that the attitudes adumbrated do reflect the overall opposition between the conservative and Liberal consensuses in America today.

A. Conservatism assumes the existence of an objective moral order based upon ontological foundations. Whether or not individual conservatives hold theistic views—and a large majority of them do—this outlook is derived from a theistic tradition. The essential point, however, is that the conservative looks at political and social questions with the assumption that there are objective standards for human conduct and criteria for the judgment of theories and institutions, which it is the duty of human beings to understand as thoroughly as they are able and to which it is their duty to approximate their actions.

The Liberal position, in contrast, is essentially operational and instrumental. As the conservative's world is, in Richard Weaver's phrase, a world of essences to be approximated, the Liberal's world is a world of problems to be solved. Hence, the conservative's concern with such questions of essence as individual liberty and civilizational tradition. Hence, the Liberal's concern with modes and operations such as democracy (a

mode or means of government which implies that what is morally right is what 50 percent plus one think is right) or progress
(a concept that derives norms from the operation of historical
events, establishing as the good the direction in which events
have been moving and seem presently to be moving).

B. Within the limits of an objective moral order, the primary
reference of conservative political and social thought and action is to the individual person. There may be among some
conservatives a greater emphasis upon freedom and rights, as
among others a greater emphasis upon duties and responsibilities; but whichever the emphasis, conservative thought is shot
through and through with concern for the person. It is deeply
suspicious of theories and policies based upon the collectivities
that are the political reference points of Liberalism—"minorities," "labor," "the people." There may be tension between
those conservatives who stress individual freedom and those
who stress community as a fabric of individual rights and responsibilities, but both reject the ideological hypostatization of
associations of human beings into entities and the collectivist
politics based upon it.

C. The cast of American conservative thought is profoundly
anti-utopian. While it recognizes the continuing historical certainty of change and the necessity of basic principle being expressed under different circumstances in different ways, and
while it strives always for the improvement of human institutions and the human condition, it rejects absolutely the idea
that society or men generally are perfectible. In particular, it is
perennially suspicious of the utopian approach that attempts
to *design* society and the lives of human beings, whether in the
light of abstract rationalist ideas or operational engineering
concepts. It therefore rejects the entire Liberal mystique of
"planning," which, no matter how humanitarian the motives
of the planners, perforce treats human beings as faceless units
to be arranged and disposed according to a design conceived
by the planner. Rather, the conservative puts his confidence in

the free functioning of the energies of free persons, individually and in voluntary cooperation.

D. It is on the basis of these last two points—concern for the individual person and rejection of utopian design—that the contemporary American conservative attitude to the state arises. For the state, which has the ultimate power of enforcement of its dictates, is the necessary implement for successful Liberal planning and for effective control of the lives of individual human beings. Conservatives may vary on the degree to which the power of the state should be limited, but they are agreed upon the principle of limitation and upon the firmest opposition to the Liberal concept of the state as the engine for the fixing of ideological blueprints upon the citizenry. There is much difference among them on the manner and mode in which the state should be limited, but in opposition to the prevailing Liberal tendency to call upon it to act in every area of human life, from automation to social relations, they are firmly united upon the principle of limitation.

E. Similarly, American conservatives are opposed to state control of the economy in all its Liberal manifestations, whether direct or indirect. They stand for a free economic system for two reasons. In the first place, they believe that the modern state is politically so strong, even without controls over the economy, that it concentrates power to a degree that is incompatible with the freedom of its citizens. When to that power is added control over the economy, such massive power is created that the last defenses against the state becoming a monstrous Leviathan begin to crack. Second—though this is subsidiary in the conservative outlook to the danger to freedom—conservatives in general believe, on the basis of classical and neoclassical economic theory, that a free economy is much more productive of material wealth than an economy controlled directly or indirectly by the state.

F. American conservatism derives from these positions its firm support of the Constitution of the United States as originally conceived—to achieve the protection of individual liberty in an ordered society by limiting the power of government. Recognizing the many different partial outlooks that went into its inception, adoption, and execution, the conservative holds that the result was a constitutional structure concerned simultaneously with limiting the power of the individual states and of the federal government, and of the tripartite elements in both—through the careful construction of a tension of separate powers, in which ultimate sovereignty rested in no single part, but in the tension itself. Conservatives believe that this conception was the closest that human beings have come to establishing a polity which gives the possibility of maintaining at one and the same time individual liberty, underlying norms of law, and necessary public order. Against the Liberal endeavor to establish sovereignty nominally in the democratic majority, actually in the executive branch of a national government, they strive to reestablish a federal system of strictly divided powers, so far as government itself is concerned, and to repulse the encroachment of government, federal or state, over the economy and the individual lives of citizens.

G. In their devotion to Western civilization and their unashamed and unself-conscious American patriotism, conservatives see Communism as an armed and messianic threat to the very existence of Western civilization and the United States. They believe that our entire foreign and military policy must be based upon recognition of this reality. As opposed to the vague internationalism and the wishful thinking about Communist "mellowing" or the value of the United Nations that characterize Liberal thought and action, they see the defense of the West and the United States as the overriding imperative of public policy.

It is difficult to summarize in a short space the consensus of a variegated and living movement, especially when it is by its very nature opposed to ideology. I have attempted, however, to

give here the best description of the contemporary American
conservative movement that I have been able to derive from
observation and experience. In confirmation of my summary, I
would present from the actual political life of the conservative
movement a statement which I think bears me out. It is the
Statement of Principles of the American Conservative Union,
founded in December 1964 with the aim of coordinating and
guiding American conservatism. I believe it states in brief compass the position I have been endeavoring to analyze, and as a
practical political document shows the essential congruity of
conservative thought with that analysis.

The American Conservative Union holds firm the truth that all
men are endowed by their Creator with unalienable rights. To a
world floundering in philosophical anarchy, we therefore com-
mend a transcendent moral order against which all human institutions, in every commonwealth, may confidently be judged.

We believe that government is meant to serve men: by securing
their rights under a rule of law that dispenses justice equally to all;
and in times of danger by marshalling the might of the commonwealth against its enemies.

We remark the inherent tendency of government to tyranny.
The prudent commonwealth will therefore labor tirelessly, by
means agreeable to its peculiar genius and traditions, to limit and
disperse the power of government. No task should be confided to a
higher authority that can be performed at a subsidiary level; and
whatever the people can do for themselves should not be confided
to government at all.

We believe that the Constitution of the United States is the ideal
charter for governing the American commonwealth. The checks
and balances that distribute the power of our national authority,
and the principle of federalism that reserves to the states or to the
people all power not confided to the national authority, are the
cornerstones of every freedom enjoyed in this commonwealth. To
their integrity we pledge a jealous defense.

We have learned that man's liberty, no less than his material interests, is promoted by an economic system based on private prop-

erty and directed by a free, competitive market. Such a system not only enlarges the scope of individual choice but by dispersing economic decisions provides a further bulwark against the concentration of political power. And no other system can assure comparable living standards and growth. As against the encroachments of the welfare state, we propose a state of welfare achieved by free, collaborative endeavor.

Today the American commonwealth, as well as the civilization that illuminated it, are mortally threatened by the global Communist revolution. We hold that permanent co-existence with Communism is neither honorable nor desirable nor possible. Communism would enslave the world by any means expedient to that end. We deem no sacrifice too great to avoid that fate. We would parry the enemy's thrusts—but more: by maintaining American military superiority and exerting relentless pressure against the Communist empire, we would advance the frontiers of freedom.

Traditionalist and Libertarian Emphases Within the Conservative Movement

There is, then, a consensus that gives the contemporary American conservative movement unity. As I argued at the beginning of this essay, it is a consensus that reflects a legitimate conservative outlook, in the sense that conservatism properly considered is not confined to the limited doctrines of the conservatism of any given historical period, but represents the effort to refresh and renew the tradition of a civilization and a nation in response to a radical challenge to that tradition. Nevertheless, although there is a conservative consensus today, there are stresses and strains within it, reflecting the differing emphases partially derived from variant strands of the tradition. Most of these stresses and strains within the conservative movement center around one fundamental clash of emphasis, that between what can be called the "traditionalist" and the "libertarian" elements within it.

The specifically American form of the Western tradition, which is the source and inspiration of contemporary American conservatism, is the consensus established by the Founding Fathers and incorporated in the constitutional settlement. While it is true that something of the tension between the traditionalist and libertarian emphases exists throughout the Western tradition and therefore exists within that consensual settlement, it had always been and remained at the time of the establishment of the Republic precisely that—a tension *within* a basic civilizational consensus. It is from that integrated foundation that the overall consensus of the American conservatism of today is built. To some degree therefore the traditionalist-libertarian opposition within it is directly derived from its source. But many of the characteristics of that opposition, characteristics often threatening the maintenance of consensus, are derived from a very different source, from the naturalization in the United States, during this century and the last part of the nineteenth century, of the nineteenth-century conflict between European conservatism and European liberalism. This is historically ironic because that European conflict was the aftermath of the French Revolution, and neither that revolution nor the system which it overthrew had relevance for the American situation. By the same token, the positions of European liberalism and European conservatism of the nineteenth century are also irrelevant here.

The philosophical position upon which the American constitutional settlement was based had already brought into a common synthesis concepts which were placed in radical opposition by the European conservative-liberal struggle: a respect for the tradition together with a respect for reason, the acceptance of the authority of an organic moral order together with a fierce concern for the freedom of the individual person. That synthesis is neither liberal nor conservative in the nineteenth-century sense. Efforts of writers like Louis Hartz to maintain that it is essentially "liberal" in either the nineteenth-century European sense or the twentieth-century American sense are based on a misunderstanding of the Constitutional consensus—as well as being historically anachronistic; and this is also true of those who would equate that consensus with the point of view of nineteenth-century European conservatism.

Nineteenth-century conservatism defended values based upon a fundamental moral order and the authority of tradition, standing firmly against the corrosive attack of utilitarianism, positivism, and scientism. But it did not recognize as a truth corollary to its defense of moral values that acceptance by individual persons of the moral authority of objective standards of the good must be voluntary; when it is a mere surface acceptance imposed by external power, it is without meaning or content. Nineteenth-century conservatism was all too willing to substitute for the authority of the good the authoritarianism of human rulers and to support an authoritarian political and social structure.

Nineteenth-century liberalism, on the other hand, stood firmly for the freedom of the individual person and, in defense of that freedom, developed the doctrine and practice of limited state power and the free economy. But as it did so, it corroded by its utilitarianism belief in an objective moral order as the foundation of respect for the value and integrity of the individual person and therefore the only firm foundation of individual freedom.

The traditionalist and the libertarian within the contemporary American conservative movement are not heirs of European conservatism and European liberalism because they draw from a common source in the American constitutional consensus. Their common effort to achieve a philosophical clarification of the consensus that underlies their actual empirical participation in the single movement is, however, impeded by the importation of the nineteenth-century European categories. As I have written elsewhere:

> The misunderstanding between libertarian and traditionalist are
> to a considerable degree the result of a failure to understand the

differing levels on which classical liberal doctrines are valid and invalid. Although the classical liberal forgot—and the contemporary libertarian conservative sometimes tends to forget—that in the *moral* realm freedom is only a means whereby men can pursue their proper end, which is virtue, he did understand that in the *political* realm freedom is the primary end. If, with Acton, we "take the establishment of liberty for the realization of moral duties to be the end of civil society," the traditionalist conservative of today, living in an age when liberty is the last thought of our political mentors, has little cause to reject the contributions to the understanding of liberty of the classical liberals, however corrupted their understanding of the ends of liberty. Their error lay largely in the confusion of the temporal with the transcendent. They could not distinguish between the *authoritarianism* with which men and institutions suppress the freedom of men, and the *authority* of God and truth.[1]

The divergent emphases of traditionalist and libertarian are, however, gradually being resolved in the life of the American conservative movement. Several factors contribute to this resolution: common action in the political struggle against Liberalism, a conscious return to a study of the founding tradition of the Republic, and a deepening of contemporary conservative thought itself.

Problems of the American Conservative Movement

The deepening of conservative thought, however, is only at its beginnings. This is understandable, because in the dozen years or so that this conscious conservative movement has been in existence, its first intellectual task has been to fight for recognition as a legitimate position in an intellectual climate of conformity to Liberal norms. A movement striving to gather its

1. "Freedom, Tradition, Conservatism," in *What Is Conservatism?*, ed. Frank S. Meyer (New York: Holt, Rinehart and Winston, 1964), 15–16 (24).

forces in a hostile environment will quite naturally tend in the first instance to concentrate upon the simple statement and restatement of its basic principles, and upon elaborating those principles only insofar as it is necessary to sustain a critique of the principles and practices against which the movement is arrayed. When, following such a primary period of constitution, the intellectual sector of such a movement finds itself rather suddenly and somewhat unexpectedly involved in a serious political development like the Goldwater surge of 1960 to 1964, there arises an overwhelming temptation to turn aside from further development of fundamental thought and occupy itself with practical political questions of skills and techniques. It is true that the skills and techniques of political organization are essential to the success of a political movement and that conservatives have only recently begun to cultivate them; but they are only auxiliaries for a movement which, by its nature, stands for nothing less than a radical transformation of the consciousness of an age.

This is what the contemporary American conservative movement exists to do. It has no other excuse for being. Concentration on method, without greater emphasis on transforming consciousness, could lead only to practical political rivalry with Liberalism on its own grounds. Such a development of conservatism would end by making it a right wing of the Liberal consensus, not a challenge to its essence. The conservative movement in coming into being has set itself a greater and much more difficult task: to appeal to the civilizational instincts and beliefs that it feels survive half-smothered in the American people. But this cannot be done except upon the basis of a broad and profound development of the conservative world-view.

That task is complex. Although, simply stated, the world-view of conservatism is the world-view of Western civilization, conservatism in a revolutionary age cannot be content with pious repetition of a series of received opinions. Too much has been shattered for it to be possible ever merely to return to the forms and modes of the past. Conservatism needs to be more than preservative; its function is to restore, and to do so by creating new forms and modes to express, in contemporary circumstances, the essential content of Western civilization. To do this it cannot confine itself to a broad attack upon established Liberalism. It has to meet the pretensions of Liberalism area by area and point by point at the level that *conservative* pretensions to be the heirs of Western civilization demand. This requires nothing less than a critical appraisal of the corpus of the intellectual activity of the twentieth century with the aim of applying ageless principles to it and thereby deepening those principles.

This is a task of which conservative scholars are becoming more and more aware. Nor would I want to give the impression that a good deal of work in this direction has not already been done. I emphasize the task, however, because upon a serious endeavor to fulfill it depends the growth to maturity of the American conservative movement.

Another problem corollary to this one, or more accurately derivative from it, confronts conservatism on a more immediate practical level. What I am referring to is the translation of conservative principles into specific alternatives to the accepted Liberal public policies. The weakness here is one of execution, a weakness which could be characteristic of any young and fresh movement and is not generically a conservative weakness. There is, however, a difficulty in overcoming it that derives from the underlying political stance of conservatism as compared with the stance of Liberalism and from the tone of approach to social and political problems that prevails today because of the influence of Liberalism. Liberalism finds in every social situation problems to be collectively solved by planned action, usually action involving the use of the power of government. Conservatism considers some of these situations natural manifestations of the human spirit and not "problems" to be solved at all; others it recognizes as situations that can be improved, but only by time and the working of free human energies individually or in voluntary association; above all, it considers the greatest social and political problem the increasing provenance and power of the state and therefore considers a further increase of that provenance and power a greater evil than the specific evils against which the state is called into action.

Since regnant Liberalism creates an atmosphere in which positive solutions to every conceivable problem are demanded, to be "negative" is the greatest of sins. But if conservatism is to be true to its vision, a large portion of its program will be negative insofar as proposing governmental action to remedy social situations is concerned. It will propose the limitation of government in order to free the energies of citizens to go about remedying these situations in their several ways as they see best. In the Liberal atmosphere this can easily be made to sound callous, hard-hearted, uncaring. But to maintain that hardships, deprivations, social imbalances are not properly or effectively solved by state action is not to deny their existence. Rather it is to call upon the imaginative exercise of voluntary altruistic effort to restore a widespread sense of responsibility for social well-being and to guard against the moral degradation of citizens as direct clients of the state or as indirect petitioners for community largesse.

Some examples of what can be done may be seen in the recent work of the Foundation for Voluntary Welfare, headed by Richard C. Cornuelle. It has already brought to completion one project and begun another, each of which is directed to the remedy of social situations through voluntary effort. The United Student Aid Fund has already been established through the agency of the Foundation for Voluntary Welfare, with the assistance of bankers, businessmen, and administrators, to preempt a large part of the field of loans to students, which would otherwise have become an additional activity of expanding government. Mr. Cornuelle's next project is to take Marion County, Indiana, as a pilot community and there to enlist all available private resources in an all-out attempt to eliminate hard-core unemployment in that county.

This is conservative action of a kind which cannot be incorporated in a neat "positive program" for the political arena (similarly, the enormous constructive thrust of private industry, which we have come to take for granted, does not lend itself to neat political packaging). But such action could and would be multiplied a thousandfold if a conservatively directed citizenry ceased to look to government and if the corollary shrinkage of government left in the hands of the citizens resources now taxed from them to support government programs.

But even when the charge of callousness to human distress is countered, the charge of negativity still remains. The only answer conservatives can make to this charge, unless they wish to descend to unprincipled demagogy, is to show that a positive program for the preservation of freedom and the expansion of human energies requires a series of negative programs directed towards the dismantling of smothering governmental activities. Such a program can be effectively presented only if it analyzes compellingly and specifically the actuality of government activities area by area; otherwise, no matter how generally correct the criticism, it gives the impression of being merely destructive criticism. It is here that the conservative movement still lacks fully adequate programmatic development. It needs studies, such as those of Martin Anderson on urban renewal, of Arnold W. Green on governmental programs for the young, the old, for recreation, for automation, or of Roger A. Freeman on federal aid to education, in every field where Liberalism invokes state action. And further, it needs to develop means of effectively transmitting the conclusions of such studies to the electorate. Only in a few areas, such as national defense or the handling of crime, where government is the natural organ for positive action, can conservative programs be intrinsically "positive." Here, too, a great deal more development of general conservative positions is needed.

Such specification of a conservative program, negative or positive, is as necessary as the deepening and enriching of conservative thought on a higher level, which I discussed earlier. Until it is done, the statement of sharp conservative principle, which obviously demands deep-going change in the existing situation, can sound like irresponsible radicalism. If it is not backed up by a sober, specific, and conservatively restrained program of gradually phased transformation, the considered conservative position on limited government and resistance to Communism is in danger of being translated into such nightmares as the immediate cutting off of every Social Security check or the instigation of nuclear war against the Soviet Union.

Both in fundamental thought and in practical programmatics, the present need of the American conservative movement is to intensify its development. Its essential principles are clear; they constitute a doctrine that is truly conservative in that it is directed towards the recovery of the civilizational tradition. Its future depends upon its ability to deepen its understanding of those principles and achieve full maturity.

PART FOUR

CODA

Western Civilization: The Problem of Political Freedom

Western civilization arose in southern and western Europe on the ruins of the Roman empire, the final political form of Classical civilization. It is and has always been unique among the great civilizations of the past five thousand years, whose existence is the substance of recorded history. It is unique not simply in the sense that each civilization—the Egyptian or Chinese or Classical—is manifestly different from all the others, but in a much more profound sense. In its most important characteristics it stands apart not merely from each of them but from all of them; it is differentiated from them by almost as sharp a leap as differentiated the other civilizations from the precivilization cultures of the Neolithic age. This is, I know, a disconcerting, even a shocking, statement by the standards of the cultural relativism that prevail in twentieth-century historical thought. I can only ask my readers to bear with me while I attempt to sustain it with a brief discussion of the civilizational history of mankind and the place of the West in the sweep of that history.

The significance of any civilizational order derives from the

Reprinted from *Modern Age* (Spring 1968): 120–28, by permission.

way in which it organizes the life and outlook of the individual persons who compose it in their relations to the universe in which they live—that is, in the way it relates the person to moral values, spiritual forces, the material environment, the other persons who make up the society. The various civilizations have done this in discernible styles. It is that style which defines their specific character.

For the first twenty-five hundred years of recorded history men lived in civilizations of similar styles, a style for which the Egyptian may stand as the type. These cosmological[1] civilizations conceived of existence so tightly unified and compactly fashioned that there was no room for distinction and contrast between the individual person and the social order, between the cosmos and human order, between heaven and earth, between what is and what ought to be. God and king, the rhythms of nature and the occupations of men, social custom and the moral imperative, were felt not as paired opposites but as integral unities. The life of men in these civilizations, in good times and bad, in happiness and unhappiness, proceeded in harmony and accord with nature, which knows no separation between what is and what ought to be, no tension between order and freedom, no striving of the person for individuation or the complement of that striving, the inner personal clash between the aspirations of the naked self and the moral responsibilities impressed by the very constitution of being.

Exceptions, modifications, to this basic mode of human life there undoubtedly were. Man in his essence has always been, as Aristotle long ago saw, part animal, part spiritual. The clash at the center of his nature was never totally stilled. We have in-

---

1. I take this term from Eric Voegelin's epoch-making *Order and History*, 3 vols. (Baton Rouge: Louisiana State University Press, 1956–57). I owe as well the concept that underlies this section to his work, but—as I have said previously in my *In Defense of Freedom* (Chicago: Henry Regnery, 1962)—I have developed that concept according to my own lights and he is certainly not responsible for the result.

deed documents from Mesopotamia and Egypt which show the stirrings of the impulses that shaped later ages. Nevertheless these are but stirrings; they do not express the age or affect the essential character of the cosmological civilization. They are but premonitions of what is to come.

When it came, it came with historic suddenness. It came in different ways and for different reasons among two peoples of two new civilizations—the Greeks of Classical civilization and the Jews of the Syriac civilization. The way of its coming was as different as the character of these two peoples was different, but the new understanding was in essence the same. It shattered the age-old identity of the historic and the cosmic. It burst asunder the unity of what ought to be and what is. It faced individual men for the first time with the necessity of deep-going moral choice. In a word, it destroyed the unity of what is done by human beings and what they should do to reach the heights their nature opens to them. And, in doing so, this understanding created, for the first time, the conditions for individuation, for the emergence of the person as the center of human existence, by separating the immanent from the transcendent, the immemorial mode of living from its previous identity with the very constitution of being. The arrangements of society were dissociated from the sanction of ultimate cosmic necessity; they were desanctified and left open to the judgment of human beings. But that transcendent sanction remained the basis of the judgment of human life. The transcendent was not destroyed; it was reaffirmed in terms more profound and awesome than ever. The earthly immanent and the transcendent heavenly remained, but how now were they to be related each to each?

The nexus, the connecting link between the transcendent and the immanent, between the eternal and the historical, could be no other than the human person. Living in both worlds, subjected by the demands of his nature to transcendent value and at the same time maker of history and master of society, he was suddenly (suddenly as historical process goes) revealed to himself as a creature whose fate it was to bridge this newly yawning gulf.

I am not saying, of course, that the multitudes who made up Hellenic and Judaic society thought in these terms or even dimly glimpsed them conceptually. I do maintain two things: first, that the inspirers of the two societies, the prophets of Judah and Israel and the philosophers of Greece, grasped this new condition of mankind, grasped it in fear and trembling, and, secondly, that their understanding shaped the enduring *ethos* of their societies as surely as the *ethos* of the Pharaoh God-King shaped the society of Egypt.

This common understanding of the Judaic and Hellenic cultures was expressed, of course, in radically different forms—so different, indeed, that these cultures have been more commonly conceived as polar opposites than as different expressions of the same stupendous insight. This is not to deny what is sharply opposed in the two cultures, most especially their different understandings of the relationship of man to the transcendent. But the overriding fact is that in both these cultures, at their highest level, there emerged a clear distinction between the world and the transcendent, as well as the startlingly new concept of a direct relationship between men and the transcendent.

In the Hellenic civilization it was the philosophical movement culminating with Socrates, Plato, and Aristotle that raised to the level of consciousness this new understanding of the nature of men and their relations to ultimate things. The sense of the individual, the person as over against society, had been inherent in the *ethos* of the Greeks from the dim beginnings of Hellenic civilization. Such a sense is apparent already in Hesiod and Homer. It inspires the human scale of their archaic temples, as contrasted with the monstrous inhumanity of scale of ziggurat, pyramid, and sphinx. But this inherent tendency of the Greek spirit did not, for a number of reasons, decisively shape Hellenic society. In the beginning, in the Northern war bands from which it arose, the collectivity of the pack contended always against the individual spirit; also, from that heritage it drew a religious practice and a pantheon of gods almost devoid of transcendence. Further, Hellenic civilization developed in its youth under the looming influence of the great cosmological civilizations of the East, and when the aridity of its inherited pantheon drove men to search further, the mystery religions which arose were saturated through and through with Eastern concepts. Finally, when the civilization reached maturity, the classical social form it assumed was the *polis*, the city-state, which was a tight unity of society, government, and religion. Despite the fact that within that form there was immeasurably greater room for the development of the individual personal consciousness than in the older civilizations, the shadow of the past and the limiting shackles of the life of the *polis* smothered and distorted the full emergence of the new consciousness.

It was the contradiction between the inherent Hellenic awakening to the possibilities of a new state of being and the trammels of the inherited old with which the Greek philosophers wrestled. What they created out of their struggles was the first systematic *intellectual* projection of an independent relationship between free men and transcendent value. (I stress "intellectual" because nearly simultaneously, in the Israel and Judah of the Prophetic age, there emerged another form of the same understanding, expressed not in intellectual but in existential and historic terms—a development I shall be discussing shortly.) The power and analytical depth of the Hellenic intellectual achievement were so great and profound that it has remained ever since a firm foundation for the philosophical and political thought of men who have been concerned with the freedom of the person and the authority of transcendent truth. But, as essential as the work of the Hellenic philosophers has been to the growth of this understanding, they were limited and their thought was distorted by two factors. Their limitation and distortion prevented, particularly in their political theory, the fullest confrontation with the radical independence of human beings before earthly institutions, their dependence only upon the transcendent. Of these two factors, the first, the problem of what might be called Utopianism, is best considered after we have discussed the Judaic Prophetic experience, since it is a factor that affects it as well as the Hellenic philosophical experience. The second factor was the effect of the life of the *polis* upon the consciousness of the Greek philosopher.

The mode of being of men living in the *polis* was effectively constrained by the character of that community. As I have said, the *polis* was at once state, society, and religious cult, all wrapped up in one. The citizen of such a state was truly, as Aristotle called him, "a political animal," that is, an animal of the *polis*. It was the *polis* that gave him stature; outside of it, he was only potentially human. Such men the Greeks called "barbarians"—making little distinction between uncivilized tribal peoples and the subjects of the great civilized empires of the Middle East.

There was reason in this disdain in which the men of the *polis* held the cosmological civilizations of the Middle East. Although the form of the *polis* stood between its citizens and their full achievement of freedom by independent individual confrontation of the transcendent realm of value, it did so in a different way and to a far less degree than did the cosmological societies. Hellas had broken loose from a world in which human existence was completely absorbed in the cosmos, in which the earthly and the transcendent were so merged that the person could not stand free, clearly and sharply delineated from the surrounding universe. But this new consciousness of the Hellenic spirit was bound still by the necessity of expressing itself through a collectivity—no longer the cosmic collectivity of the Middle East, but a socio-political collectivity, the *polis*.

It was, indeed, a great leap forward towards men's consciousness of their personhood and their freedom, because now the limiting form on individual freedom and individual confrontation of transcendent destiny was a collectivity composed of the subjective spirit of men, not the objective, totally external, force of iron cosmic fatality. Nevertheless, the Hellenic philosophers who expressed this spirit at its highest level always had to struggle, in their farthest penetrations towards the meaning of human existence, against the circumstances of being and thought created by *polis* society.

The Judaic experience was extraordinarily parallel to the Hellenic, although its content was very different. The Hebrew prophets, like the Greek philosophers, expressed, at the highest level, the consciousness of a people broken loose from cosmological civilization to confront transcendence. As *Exodus* is the symbol of that breaking away, the content of the Judaic experience of transcendence is the belief in a unique, personal, revealed God.

But here also, as among the Greeks, a social structure distorted the individual experience of transcendence. The potentialities for full individuation inherent in the concept of a God of Righteousness were collectivized. The concept of the *b'rith*, the compact between God and the Chosen People, placed the collectivity of the Judaic people, rather than the individuals who made up that collectivity, as the receptor of the interchange with transcendence. The Prophets strove mightily with these circumstances, as the Greek philosophers struggled with the circumstances of the *polis*. Future events have taken from them both an inspiration and an understanding that are derived from the thrust of their struggle towards individuation, but neither the philosophy of Hellas nor the prophecy of Israel ever completely threw off the conditioning influence of their social and intellectual heritage.

At the heights of the philosophical and Prophetic endeavors, in a Plato or a proto-Isaiah, as occasionally among their predecessors and followers, the vision cleared and a simple confrontation between individual men and transcendence stood for a moment sharply limned. But at these heights of understanding another problem arose, one I have referred to above when discussing the Hellenic experience and have called the problem of Utopianism. A clear vision of the naked confrontation of individual men with transcendence created a yawning gap in human consciousness. It was something of the effect of eating the fruit of the Tree of the Knowledge of Good and Evil. On the one hand stood the perfection of transcendence, and on the other the imperfection of human existence. The temptation was enormous to close that intolerable gap, to grasp that understood transcendent perfection and by sheer human will to make it live on earth, to impose it on other human beings— by persuasion if possible, by force if necessary.

The same temptation beset the Hellenic philosophers at their highest reach of vision. The effect of this temptation was portentous for the future, because of its continuing impact upon both the Hellenic and the Judaic traditions, the twin sources from which our Western civilization derives so much of its content. Its effects can be perceived in the most diverse areas: in the effect on Western thought of the concepts of moulding human life implicit in the Utopian society of Plato's *Republic* or in the dictatorial powers of the Nocturnal Council in his somewhat less rigid *Laws*; or in the actual political absolutism, derived from the Judaic tradition, of such polities as Calvin's Geneva or Spain of the Inquisition or Cromwell's England. Secularized with the passage of time, the Utopian desire to impose a pattern of what the imposers considered perfection becomes ever more rigid, total, and terrible, as in the all-powerful Nation of the French Revolution or the Dictatorship of the Proletariat of the Communists.

The Utopian temptation arises out of the very clarity of vision that tore asunder the cosmological world-view. Released from the comforting, if smothering, certainties of identification with the cosmic order, men became aware of their freedom to shape their destiny—but with that freedom came an awesome sense of responsibility. For the same leap forward that made them fully conscious of their own identity and their own freedom made them conscious also of the infinite majesty and beauty of transcendence and of the criterion of existence that perfection puts before human beings, who in their imperfection possess the freedom to strive to emulate perfection. A yawning gulf was opened between infinity and finity.

There are two possible human reactions to the recognition of this reality.

On the one hand, it can be accepted in humility and pride—humility before the majesty of transcendence and pride in the freedom of the human person. That acceptance requires willingness to live life on this earth at high tension, a tension of men conscious simultaneously of their imperfection and of their freedom and their duty to move towards perfection. The acceptance of this tension is the distinguishing characteristic of the Western civilization of which we are a part, a characteristic shared by no other civilization in the world's history.

On the other hand, the hard and glorious challenge of reality can be rejected. The tension between perfection and imperfection can be denied. Men conscious of the vision of perfection, but forgetting that their vision is distorted by their own imperfection, can seek refuge from tension by trying to impose their own limited vision of perfection upon the world. This is the Utopian temptation. It degrades transcendence by trying to set up as perfect what is by the nature of reality imperfect. And it destroys the freedom of the individual person by forcing upon him conformity to someone else's limited human vision, robbing him of freedom to move towards perfection in the tension of his imperfection. It is in form a return to the womb of the cosmological civilization, in which the tension of life at the higher level of freedom was not required of men, in which they could fulfill their duties in uncomplicated acceptance of the rhythms of the cosmos, without the pain or the glory of individuation. But Utopianism is only similar to cosmological civilizations in form; in essence it is something different, because cosmological civilization was, as it were, a state of innocence, while Utopianism comes after the eating of the fruit of the Tree of Knowledge of the persons of God and men. It is a deliberate rejection of the high level at which it is now possible for men to live, and as such it distorts and oppresses the human spirit. Yet it has remained, ever since the Hellenic and Judaic break through the cosmological crust, an ever-prevalent historical factor. In particular, as Western civilization is the civilization that accepts and lives with the tension of spirit, Utopianism has been a constantly recurring destructive force within it.

Indeed, the history of Western civilization is the history of the struggle to carry forward its insight of tension, both against the remaining inherited traumas of the cosmological attitude in its social structure and in its intellectual outlook and against the continuing recrudescence of Utopianism. For Western civilization inherited, as the Hellenic and Judaic did before it, much continuing influence from the long eons of cosmological life. And, although the forms of its thought and the content of its spirit rise directly out of the Hellenic and the Judaic themselves, it broke as far beyond them as they broke beyond the cosmological civilization. It founded itself, in its inmost core, on acceptance of the tension between the transcendent and the individual human person and on the reconciliation of that tension implicit in the great vision of the Incarnation—the flash of eternity into time.

The history of Western civilization, since it came into being out of the fermenting remnants left behind by the death of Classical civilization, is distinguished by a preeminent regard for the person. This is not to say that this regard has always, or indeed generally, been ideally reflected in its institutions and social reality; but it is to insist that, at the heart of the concept of being that forms the limiting notions by which the West has lived, the preeminence of the person has prevailed. And this is true of no previous civilization. It is of course a concept, a view of reality, at the opposite end of the scale from that of the cosmological civilizations. But it also goes radically beyond the intermediate experience of the Hellenic and Judaic civilizations. Although they, each in its own way, broke through the cosmological unity, they did so not in the name of the person as such but rather in the name of collectivities of persons, the *polis* and the Chosen People.

It was given to the West to drive to fruition the insights glimpsed in Greece and Israel. Its consciousness founded upon the symbol of the Incarnation placed the person at the center of being. From this very deepening of the understanding of the person there arises, even more than in Greece and Israel, a Utopian temptation; and that Utopianism has been expressed right down to our own day in more and more extreme forms. But while the factors we have discussed, which lead to Utopianism, are by the very nature of the Western concept of transcendence more intense than ever before, the symbol of the Incarnation that has made possible that concept and the temptation ensuing therefrom, also offers a resolution of the pressures leading to Utopianism, a resolution that did not exist in Greece and Israel. The simultaneous understanding that there exists transcendent perfection and that human beings are free and responsible to move towards perfection, although incapable of perfection, no longer puts men in an intolerable dilemma: the dilemma either, on the one hand, of denying their freedom and their personhood and sinking back into cosmological annihilation within a pantheistic All, or on the other hand of trying by sheer force of will to rival God and, as Utopians, to impose a limited human design of perfection upon a world by its nature imperfect. The Incarnation, understood as the "flash of eternity into time," the existential unity of the perfect and the imperfect, has enabled men of the West to live

both in the world of nature and in the transcendent world
without confusing them. It has made it possible to live, albeit in
a state of tension, accepting both transcendence and the human condition with its freedom and imperfection.

It is that tension which is the distinguishing mark of Western
civilization. Of course, to say that for the West alone has it been
possible to live in that state of tension, to rise above both cosmic absorption and the temptation of Utopianism, is not to say
that either the men of the West or the institutions of the West
have always, or even generally, existed at the heights that were
open to them. It is only to say that in our civilization alone has
such a conquest of these twin pitfalls of human history been
possible. Further, it is to say that the direction of the understanding of the West has been towards a grasp of this insight,
that the institutions of the West at their best reflected it, and
that the men of the West at their highest moments were inspired by it. The West has strayed often, indeed constantly, towards the fleshpots of cosmic authoritarianism, as towards the
false paradise of Utopianism. The history of the straying in the
one and the other direction is the history of the West. But always there remained in the reservoirs of Western consciousness a solution not given to other civilizations, a way out from
the impasse of previous human history, the way of its genius—
life at the height of tension.

The characteristic concepts, institutions, and style of the
West, where they stand in the sharpest contrast to those of
other civilizations, are shot through and through with tension.
And this is true from the most matter-of-fact levels of existence
to the most exalted. Everywhere, impossible contradictions
maintain themselves to create the most powerful and noble ex-
tensions of the Western spirit. At the most mundane level, the
economic, the Western credit system takes leave of hard matter, etherealizing money, the very foundation of production
and exchange. The Gothic cathedral, thrusting to the heavens,
denies the weighty stone of which it is built, while rising from

the center of its city it affirms the beauty of materiality. The doctrine of the Lateran Council, central to the philosophical tradition of the West, proclaimed, after a thousand years of intellectual effort, the pure tension of the Incarnational unity, in radical differentness, of the material and the transcendent. This is the mode of the West at its highest and most typical. But always the human heritage of the cosmological civilizations has pressed upon it, distorting its understanding, exerting a pull dragging it down from the height of its vision.

Nowhere was the effect of this force more profound in stifling and destroying the development of the Western genius than in the political sphere. It is here that the vision of the West should have been translated into actual relations of power that would have made the revolt from cosmologism real through and through the lives of individual men.

The state in the cosmological civilizations, reflecting the overall world-view of these civilizations, was the sanctified symbol of the cosmos. In it resided both earthly and transcendent meaning, unified in a grand power that left to the individual person little meaning or value beyond that which adhered to him as a cell of the whole.

In radical contrast, the vision of the West, splitting asunder the transcendent and the earthly, placed their meeting point in tension, in the souls of individual men. The individual person became, under God, the ultimate repository of meaning and value. That world-view demanded a consonant political structure, one in which the person would be primary and all institutions—in particular the state—secondary and derivative. But Western civilization in Europe never achieved this in serious measure, either in practice or in theory. The continuing heritage of cosmologism, which again and again, in all spheres, arose to resist, weaken, and destroy the Western vision, here, in the political sphere, combined with the natural lust of men for power to maintain in large measure the age-old sanctification of the state as enforcer of virtue.

The Western spirit broke through, of course, so that neither the state nor thought about the state was purely cosmological. In their thought, Christian men could never fully divinize the state; and in their practice, they early created two sets of tensions which divided power, thus effectively preventing the full reemergence of the cosmological state and creating room for the existence of the person to a degree impossible in cosmological civilization. Those two sets of tensions were, on the one hand, the separate centers of power represented by the Church and secular political power—empire or monarchy— and, on the other hand, the broad decentralization of secular power inherent in the feudal system. Nevertheless, both the holders of hierarchical churchly power and of secular power (first, the Holy Roman Emperors and then the emerging territorial monarchs) moved with all their strength to reestablish cosmological unity. The inner spirit of the West resisted and for long centuries the issue swayed back and forth in the balance. Only, indeed, in the sixteenth, seventeenth, and eighteenth centuries, with the subordination of church (whether Protestant or Catholic) to state, with the increasing subordination of feudal and local rights to central authority, with the emergence of the absolutist monarchies of Bourbon, Tudor, and Habsburg, was the Western drive towards diversity and separation of powers tamed. But never, in fact, was cosmologism, even in the political sphere, established in the West. It took cosmologism's twin, Utopianism, in the form of the mass egalitarian nationalism of the French Revolution, to make the decisive break towards mystical statism, to sow a harvest which was fully reaped by the totalitarianisms of the twentieth century.

All this is not to maintain that the political forms of the West were ever in a deep sense cosmological or even that the Utopian state in its grim parody of cosmologism, approached totalism until the emergence of the Communism and Nazism of our time. It is, however, to assert that Western civilization in its European experience did not achieve political institutions fully coherent with its spirit.

Likewise, the basic thrust of Western political theory on the European continent (and in England, though to a lesser degree) was bound always within the categories of the Hellenic philosophers and the Hebrew prophets. Neither of these influences allowed the expression of the full drive of the Western spirit towards the primacy of the person and the limitation of political powers. The one, bounded by the *polis,* could only conceive of full freedom of the person in the emancipated flight of the philosopher beyond temporal conditions; the other, inheriting the concept of the Chosen People—even when it enlarged that concept to all humanity in the manner of a proto-Isaiah, could grasp the freedom of the person only in other-worldly relationships between man and God. Both the Hebrew and the Hellenic influences bore strongly against the development of a political philosophy that would provide the basis for a political structure solidly based on the primacy of the person and directed towards achieving the greatest possible freedom of the person.

It is true that the underlying *ethos* of the West again and again moved in this direction. Much of the thought of medieval political philosophers and legal theorists, some of the arguments of writers on both sides of the Papal-Imperial struggle, the tradition of the common law of England, drive in this direction. But these efforts, while they broke ground for the future, never rose to the creation of a truly Western political philosophy of freedom. And when, in the ferment that culminated in the French Revolution, it seemed as though such a concept might break through, it was swallowed up in the communitarian outlook typified by Rousseau, in the egalitarianism of the collective Nation, and by the Revolution itself and the nationalisms that followed in its wake throughout the continent.

In England, both in practice and in theory, there arose out of the conflicts of the seventeenth century and the relaxation of the eighteenth, something closer to a society of personal freedom and limited government. But the drag of established ideas, institutions, and power held that society back from achieving the political potentiality towards which it was moving.

Thus the stage was set, when the American experience reached its critical point and the United States was constituted. The men who settled these shores and established an extension of Western civilization here carried with them the heritage of the centuries of Western development. With it they carried the contradiction between the driving demands of the Western *ethos* and a political system inconsonant with that *ethos*. In the open lands of this continent, removed from the overhanging presence of cosmological remains, they established a constitution that for the first time in human history was constructed to guarantee the sanctity of the person and his freedom. But they brought with them also the human condition, which is tempted always by the false visions of Utopianism.

The establishment of a free constitution is the great achievement of America in the drama of Western civilization. The struggle for its preservation against Utopian corrosion is the continuing history of the United States since its foundation, a struggle which continues to this day and which is not yet decided.

Bibliographical Essay

Frank S. Meyer was a prolific writer of short essays and political and philosophical commentaries. He also wrote two books, *The Moulding of Communists: The Training of the Communist Cadre* (New York: Harcourt, Brace, 1961) and the work reprinted here, *In Defense of Freedom: A Conservative Credo*, first published by Henry Regnery Company of Chicago in 1962. Meyer collected his best shorter articles in *The Conservative Mainstream* (New Rochelle, N.Y.: Arlington House, 1969). The posthumously published *Breathes There the Man: Heroic Ballads and Poems of the English-Speaking Peoples* (LaSalle, Ill.: Open Court, 1973) was edited by Meyer with the assistance of Jared Lobdell. Meyer, a singer of the great songs of the Western world, dedicated this little-known book "To the American Soldiers Who Fell in Indochina."

The principal argument of Meyer's writings is that proponents of traditional conservatism and libertarianism should cooperate toward a "fusion" of their respective views. This belief accounted for much of the polemical literature about his writings. For example, Meyer's examination of the traditionalist views of Russell Kirk in his essay "Collectivism Rebaptized" (*Freeman*, July 1955) provoked numerous responses from leading figures of the American Right, some of whom would deem Meyer's essay to be an attack, not an examination. Meyer said that "Freedom, Tradition, Conservatism" (*Modern Age*, Fall

1960) was his "most systematic analysis" of the tensions in modern conservatism. This essay was later included in *What Is Conservatism?* (New York: Holt, Rinehart and Winston, 1964), a book published for the Intercollegiate Studies Institute. A complementary essay, "A Conservative Case for Freedom," by M. Stanton Evans may be found in *Modern Age* (Fall 1960). Murray Rothbard responded to both essays in "Conservatism and Freedom: A Libertarian Comment" (*Modern Age*, Spring 1961). Rothbard's other assessments of Meyer's writings are in "Frank S. Meyer: The Fusionist as Libertarian Manqué" (*Modern Age*, Fall 1981). Meyer replied to Rothbard in "Libertarianism or Libertinism" (*National Review*, September 9, 1969).

Meyer wrote a defense of John Stuart Mill in reply to a critical essay, "Mill's 'On Liberty' Reconsidered," by Russell Kirk (*National Review*, January 25, 1956). Meyer's essay, "In Defense of John Stuart Mill" (*National Review*, March 28, 1956) was expanded upon in "Conservatives in Pursuit of Truth" (*National Review*, June 6, 1956).

Another important exchange consisted of "Conservatism and Crisis: A Reply to Father Parry" (*Modern Age*, Winter 1962–63), a response to Father Stanley Parry's "The Restoration of Tradition" (*Modern Age*, Spring 1961). Father Parry, in return, reviewed *In Defense of Freedom* in "The Face of Freedom" (*Modern Age*, Spring 1964). A year later, just before the publication of *In Defense of Freedom*, Meyer responded to an essay by L. Brent Bozell, "Freedom or Virtue?" with "Why Freedom" (both essays appearing in *National Review*, September 25, 1962). Some of the differences of view between leading figures of the time are summarized in a series of responses under the title "Do It Yourself Conservatism" (*National Review*, January 30, 1962). These exchanges, by M. Morton Auerbach, M. Stanton Evans, Russell Kirk, and Meyer, had been prompted by Evans's review of Professor Auerbach's *The Conservative Illusion*.

A noteworthy and rather acerbic exchange on the meaning of conservatism was between Meyer and Donald Atwell Zoll in the pages of *National Review*. In sequence, the exchange included Zoll's "Shall We Let America Die?" (December 16, 1969); Meyer's "What Kind of Order?" (December 30, 1969), an essay in which Meyer wrote that the distemper of the times should be met, not by the iron state, but by civility and freedom; Zoll's "Order and Repression" (March 10, 1970); Meyer's "In Re Professor Zoll: I—Order and Freedom" (March 24, 1970); and "In Re Professor Zoll: II—Defense of the Republic" (April 7, 1970).

One of Meyer's best-known essays is "Conservatism," included in *Left, Right, and Center: Essays on Liberalism and Conservatism in the United States*, edited by Robert A. Goldwin (Chicago: Rand McNally, for the Public Affairs Conference Center of Kenyon College, Gambier, Ohio, 1967). This essay later appeared as "The Recrudescent American Conservatism" in *Did You Ever See a Dream Walking?: American Conservative Thought in the Twentieth Century*, edited by William F. Buckley, Jr. (Indianapolis: Bobbs-Merrill, 1970). This book demonstrates much of the variety of American conservative thought through a collection of some of the most noted conservative essays published between 1928 and 1970.

Near the end of his life, Meyer, strongly influenced by the writings of Eric Voegelin, embedded the thesis of *In Defense of Freedom* in an essay entitled "Western Civilization: The Problem of Political Freedom" (*Modern Age*, Spring 1968).

Other replies to, commentaries on, or reviews of Meyer's principal thesis include: "A 'Fusionist' Approach to Freedom," by John Weicher (*New Individualist Review*, Autumn 1962); "Liberalism and Neo-Conservatism: Is a Synthesis Possible?" by Ronald Hamowy (*Modern Age*, Fall 1964); "The Fusionists on Liberalism and Tradition," by Ralph Raico (*New Individualist Review*, 3, no. 3, n.d.); and "Freedom and Fusion," by Reginald D. Lang (*Individualist*, January–February 1963). Additional essays relevant to Meyer's thesis may be found in the complete *New Individualist Review* (Indianapolis: Liberty Fund, 1981).

The first edition of Meyer's *In Defense of Freedom* received major reviews by Russell Kirk, "An Ideologue of Liberty" (*Sewanee Review*, April–June 1964), and an untitled review by John Hallowell (*American Political Science Review*, September 1964). Other reviews of Meyer's *What Is Conservatism?* are "The Dualistic Answer," by Vincent Miller (*Modern Age*, Fall 1964), and "American Conservatism Today," by Felix Morley (*National Review*, March 24, 1964).

Reviews of Meyer's *The Conservative Mainstream* include "The Drift to Starboard," by Stephen J. Tonsor (*Modern Age*, Summer 1969), and "The Old Man in the Back of the Room," by William F. Buckley, Jr. (*National Review*, March 25, 1969). An important related essay is "Conservatism and Libertarianism: The Common Ground," by Richard M. Weaver (*Individualist*, May 1960), reprinted in Weaver's *Life Without Prejudice* (Chicago: Henry Regnery, 1965). Meyer reflects on Weaver's influence on his own work and on the close intellectual alliance between the two men, in "Richard M. Weaver: An Appreciation" (*Modern Age*, Summer–Fall 1970). For a later look at many of the issues involved in these controversies, see *Freedom and Virtue: The Conservative/Libertarian Debate*, by George W. Carey (Lanham, Md.: University Press of America, 1984). Paul Gottfried provides a shorter retrospective in "Toward a New Fusionism?" (*Policy Review*, Fall 1987).

Two preeminent studies of modern American conservatism that include considerations of Frank Meyer are *The Conservative Intellectual Movement in America Since 1945*, by George H. Nash (New York: Basic Books, 1976), and *The American Conservative Movement: The Philosophical Founders*, by John P. East (Chicago: Regnery, 1986). Though Clinton Rossiter never quite understands Meyer, he appraises his subject in *Conservatism in America: The Thankless Persuasion* (New York: Knopf, 1962). See also *Conservative Minds in America*, by Ronald Lora (Chicago: Rand McNally, 1971).

The extensive footnotes and bibliographical essay that

George Nash provides in *The Conservative Intellectual Movement* were especially helpful in compiling this collection of Meyer's essays. A useful retrospective of Meyer's influence, though critical of what the authors term Meyer's tendency to attach "cosmic implications to every issue he wrote on," is *The Conservative Movement*, by Paul Gottfried and Thomas Fleming (Boston: Twayne, 1988).

Finally, there are a few published personal portraits of Frank Meyer and also of Elsie Meyer that are well worth reading. Easily available are "Frank S. Meyer: RIP" (*National Review*, April 28, 1972) and "Elsie Meyer, RIP" (*National Review*, May 23, 1975). Remembrances of Meyer in more obscure publications include an affectionate, unsigned piece by Murray Rothbard, "Frank S. Meyer, RIP" (*Libertarian Forum*, May 1972); "The Warrior Lives On," by Jared Lobdell (*New Guard*, March 1974); "An Interview With Frank Meyer," by John Boland (*New Guard*, July/August 1975); "The Pervasive Influence of Frank Meyer," by John Chamberlain (*Human Events*, April 15, 1972); "Frank Meyer, R.I.P.," by Jameson G. Campaigne, Jr. (*Alternative*, June–September 1972); and the foreword by Edwin J. Feulner, Jr., to the Heritage Foundation's 1991 *President's Essay*. A fine short essay on Meyer's thought is "The Living Legacy of Frank S. Meyer," by David Brudnoy (*Alternative*, April 1973). Henry Regnery gracefully gives Meyer his due in his *Memoirs of a Dissident Publisher* (New York: Harcourt Brace Jovanovich, 1979).

William C. Dennis

Index

The typeface for the text of this book is Baskerville. Its creator, John Baskerville (1706–75), broke with tradition to reflect in his type the rounder, yet more sharply cut lettering of eighteenth-century stone inscriptions and copy books. The type foreshadows modern design in such novel characteristics as the increase in contrast between thick and thin strokes and the shifting of stress from the diagonal to the vertical strokes. Realizing that this new style of letter would be most effective if cleanly printed on smooth paper with genuinely black ink, he built his own presses, developed a method of hot-pressing the printed sheet to a smooth, glossy finish, and experimented with special inks. However, this typeface did not enter into general commercial use in England until 1923.

This book is printed on paper that is acid-free and meets the requirements of the American National Standard for Permanence of Paper for Printed Library Materials, Z39.48-1992. ∞

Book design by Hermann Strohbach, New York, New York
Typography by Weimer Graphics, Inc.,
Indianapolis, Indiana
Printed and bound by Worzalla Publishing Company
Stevens Point, Wisconsin